INTO THE STREETS

FOR MY PARENTS, WHO LET ME SPEAK MY MIND,
AND FOR ALL THOSE WHO RAISE THEIR VOICES FOR JUSTICE

Zest Books™
An imprint of Lerner Publishing Group, Inc.
241 First Avenue North
Minneapolis, MN 55401 USA

For reading levels and more information, look up this title at www.lernerbooks.com.
Visit us at zestbooks.net.

Main body text set in Univers LT Std 45 Light.
Typeface provided by Adobe Systems.

Library of Congress Cataloging-in-Publication Data

Names: Bieschke, Marke, author.
Title: Into the streets : a young person's visual history of protest in the United States / Marke Bieschke.
Description: Minneapolis, MN : Zest Books, [2020] | Includes bibliographical references and index. | Summary: "Prominently featured photos, artwork, and other visual elements will guide young adult readers through this lively, informative exploration of significant protests, sit-ins, and collective acts of resistance throughout US history." —Provided by publisher.
Identifiers: LCCN 2019034596 (print) | LCCN 2019034597 (ebook) | ISBN 9781541579033 (library binding) | ISBN 9781541579040 (paperback) | ISBN 9781541581463 (ebook)
Subjects: LCSH: Protest movements—United States—Juvenile literature. | Protest movements—United States—Pictorial works—Juvenile literature. | Political participation—United States—Juvenile literature. | Political participation—United States—Pictorial works—Juvenile literature.
Classification: LCC HN59.2 .B54 2020 (print) | LCC HN59.2 (ebook) | DDC 303.48/40973—dc23

LC record available at https://lccn.loc.gov/2019034596
LC ebook record available at https://lccn.loc.gov/2019034597

Manufactured in the United States of America
1-47091-47891-12/6/2019

INTO THE STREETS

A YOUNG PERSON'S VISUAL HISTORY OF PROTEST IN THE UNITED STATES

MARKE BIESCHKE

Z ZEST BOOKS
MINNEAPOLIS

CONTENTS

A RICH PAGEANT OF PROTEST AND RESISTANCE

Young people in Washington, DC, join nearly four million protesters around the world for the global climate strikes of September 2019.

March 5, 1968, started as a normal Tuesday at Garfield High School in East Los Angeles, California. Teachers were wrapping up classes for lunch. The sun shone down on the concrete playground.

Suddenly footsteps rang in the hall. Fists pounded on classroom doors. Faculty members looked up in surprise as hundreds of students rose from their desks and streamed outside, pumping their fists in the air, shouting, *"Viva la revolución"* and "Education, not eradication!"

The students were mostly Mexican American. They were protesting against the way the school system treated them. Students were forbidden to speak Spanish at school, or they would be spanked. They couldn't use the restroom during lunch. Schools refused to teach Mexican

American history and excluded Chicano students from advanced classes. Some teachers were openly racist.

"We took it upon ourselves to try and do something," said Paula Crisostomo, a junior from a nearby school whose geometry teacher had told her she would never go to college because she would probably get pregnant.

Or as Margarita Cuarón, then a sophomore, recalled, "I pick up a cone on the street. I jump on a car and start yelling, 'Walk out!'"

The protests continued throughout the week. Students from other schools joined in, until almost twenty-two thousand participated in the walkouts, known as blowouts. Although it seemed as though the blowouts were spontaneous, organizers had planned them for months, as part of the larger Chicano movement for civil rights. Students had surveyed other students to ask what concerned them most, and based on the responses, they listed their demands to the school board.

The police beat the students and panicked politicians called them a threat to the country, but their protests gained national news coverage. Eventually, the school board agreed to allow bilingual classes, a Chicano history curriculum, and funds to upgrade facilities. Young people had made a statement. Their protest transformed the education system.

WHAT IS A PROTEST?

In general, a protest is a statement or action that expresses disapproval or objection to something. This can mean voicing dissent (disagreeing with laws or commonly held attitudes), demanding that those in authority fix things, or acting directly to change a situation—such as dumping tea into Boston Harbor to stop unfair taxation or refusing to give up your bus seat because the law says Black people have to move to the back.

Besides student walkouts, protests can be massive marches, colorful demonstrations, quiet sit-ins, or wild riots. Boycotts target companies that treat workers badly or fail to follow laws. Rallies encourage people to keep fighting for better working conditions or a cleaner environment. Candlelight vigils honor the victims of preventable tragedies and help communities heal. Hashtags such as #MeToo educate people about important issues and inspire them to share their stories.

Protests can be silent, such as the annual Day of Silence in many schools that protests the treatment of LGBTQ students. Or they can be deliberately loud, drowning out messages of hate or alerting neighbors to a threat. Some turn violent, as when armed police lash out against protesters or riots destroy cities. And some are calm, as when a wave of Black students in the 1950s politely sat down in segregated cafés throughout the South and refused to leave.

Signing petitions, going on strike, coordinating email campaigns, and blocking streets . . . these are all forms of protest. And so is just standing on the corner by yourself, holding a little sign that tells the world what you think!

A Rich Pageant of Protest and Resistance

THE PURPOSE OF PROTEST

Public protest has been a vital part of US history since before the country even existed. Our founding documents guarantee the right to free speech and peaceful assembly, as well as the freedom to hold government accountable, seek better lives, protect our liberties, and pursue happiness. Speaking out and connecting with one another about what we see as unjust or unfair is how our system works.

These protesters are practicing civil disobedience—they are breaking the law deliberately but gently to make a point.

Many people assume that the only successful protests are those that cause things to change immediately. That if you're protesting a war, for example, the protest is a failure if that war doesn't end right away. This is a bit dramatic. While it's true that some of the major protests in the country's history did lead directly to big changes in law and national opinion, it was hardly a matter of just marching around for a few hours and chanting slogans. Many of these changes were the result of years of coordination and effort.

Protesting also can bring people together to share information and opinions or provide emotional support after traumatic events. It can be a release valve for bottled-up anger that would otherwise erupt into violence—a well-planned protest can channel all that energy into positive action. Protests can also show the world that some citizens disagree with what their government is doing, a powerful statement of democracy.

One of the most important functions of a protest is to draw attention to a cause. Throughout this book, you'll see the ingenious ways protests have attracted and used the media to spread the word—from rousing music and radical fashions to sophisticated press campaigns and celebrity endorsements. You'll read about processions led by fantastically dressed women riding white horses, unbelievable pranks such as attempting to levitate the Pentagon, provocative manifestos, star-studded concerts, giant quilts, total freak-outs, and stunning spectacles.

A very personal reason for protesting, even if you don't get the result you want, is to be able to say to yourself that you stood up for something you believed in. Many people take great satisfaction in exercising their rights as citizens, especially since some countries don't allow protesting at all.

NONVIOLENCE AND CIVIL DISOBEDIENCE

Protests in the United States have a long history of embracing the twin concepts of nonviolence and civil disobedience. "Civil Disobedience" was the name of a famous essay by the philosopher Henry David Thoreau, published in 1849, which argued that it was immoral to pay taxes to a government that was using the money to support slavery and wage a dishonest war against

Mexico. Even if it meant going to jail, Thoreau reasoned that breaking a bad law (such as paying taxes to a corrupt government) was better than slowly trying to change it through the normal process.

While the concept of civil disobedience is much older than the essay, Thoreau's philosophy became a touchstone for protesters that followed. Perhaps you have seen or read about protesters blocking traffic or occupying school administration or congressional offices and refusing to leave. These protesters are practicing civil disobedience—they are breaking the law deliberately but gently to make a point. They expect to be arrested and punished for their actions, which they consider a necessary price to pay for drawing attention to their cause. Causing a public fuss almost always draws media coverage. That helps amplify a protest's message.

Nonviolence is a protest strategy that considers fighting and hurting people unnecessary to create change. By avoiding violence, protesters can gain the sympathy of the public and advance their cause through education, conversation, debate, elections, and other forms of outreach and action—including civil disobedience. Nonviolence was most famously practiced by millions of people during India's struggle for independence from Britain in the early twentieth century, led by Mahatma Gandhi. Martin Luther King Jr. and the US civil rights movement embraced nonviolence. It continues to be the most common type of protest here.

ABOUT THIS BOOK

In the pages ahead, you'll see key protests that shaped US history, including everything from the violent colonial-era uprisings to contemporary social media–driven resistance campaigns. Looking over six centuries of protest, you can see certain topics turn up over and over again: racism, sexism, economic inequality, police brutality, environmental crisis, and political corruption. Slowly and with great energy, generations of protesters have chipped away at these concerns. The name of this book comes from a chant LGBTQ activists used to rouse their community to demonstrate against homophobic laws: "Out of the bars and into the streets!"

As I wrote this book, almost two million people marched on the island of Hong Kong to protect their independence from neighboring China. In the African country of Sudan, hundreds of thousands of demonstrators succeeded in changing their authoritarian government. Protesters in US cities railed against the policy of separating immigrant families at the southern border and detaining children in camps.

The world is full of thousands of acts of resistance. I hope this book inspires you to look deeper into the vibrant history of protest—and maybe plan one of your own!

CHAPTER 1

FROM PUEBLO REVOLT TO UNDERGROUND RAILROAD

EARLY AMERICAN RESISTANCE, 1492-1865

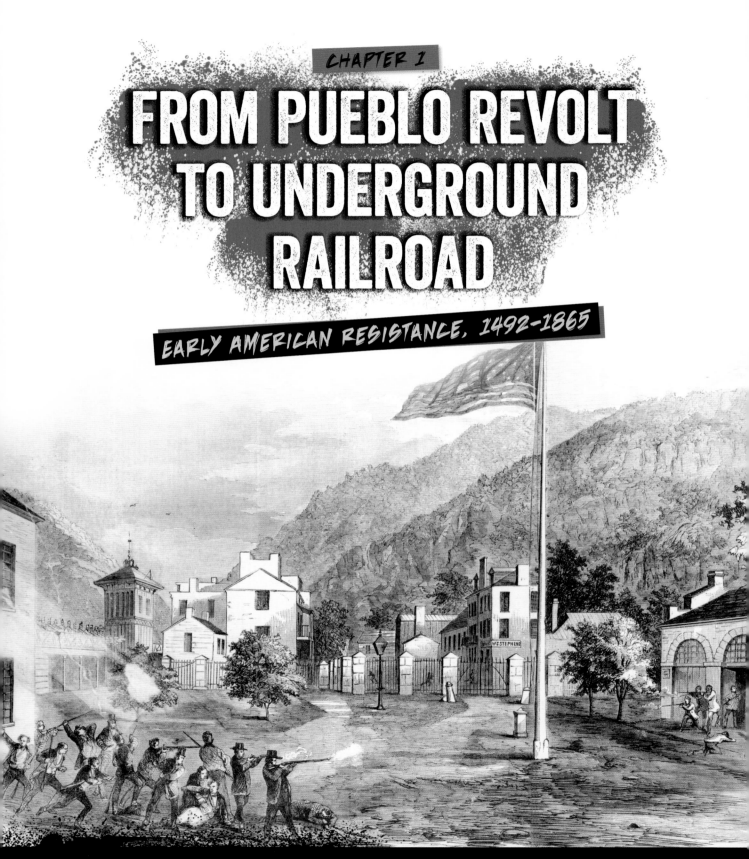

John Brown's 1859 raid on Harper's Ferry, Virginia, was a revolt against slavery.

Protest tactics in the colonial era and pre-Civil War United States take many different forms.

Acts of resistance on North American soil began almost as soon as European colonists set foot on Native American land. Little recorded history exists of the conflicts that took place before this point among indigenous communities—up to eighteen million people inhabited what became US territory in 1492. But there were surely acts of personal and intertribal resistance then too. Many Native American myths and stories, especially those featuring the trickster character Coyote, brim with rebellion.

Most early anti-colonial resistance by Native Americans took the form of violent raids and warfare. European newcomers used force to evict these original residents from their land, bringing deadly diseases and advanced weapons with them, along with a racist view that they were entitled to the "new" continent. Native Americans did what they could to repel the newcomers or at least contain their advance.

North America before the colonists was already a complex place. Not all Native nations rejected the Europeans, which caused an ever-changing web of associations and hostilities to arise. Still, pushback against the colonists, both violent and nonviolent, grew as more colonists arrived and clashed with local peoples. One nonviolent protest tactic was silence. The refusal to trade or communicate with colonists, many of whom needed guidance and goods, was one way for locals to show colonists they weren't wanted.

Other tactics were more violent. During the Pueblo Revolt of 1680, people in the Southwest collectively known as the Pueblo rose up against Spanish oppressors, who had attempted to squelch their spiritual practice and culture. Enslaved and tortured by Spaniards, who forced them to observe Catholic religious rituals and Spanish traditions, the Pueblo organized under the charismatic leader Po'pay and violently rebelled. The Pueblo killed priests, destroyed churches, and banished the Spanish from their territory.

After the United States was established in 1776, indigenous groups across the country continued to try to protect themselves. In the Midwest, Shawnee leaders Tecumseh and his brother Tenskwatawa united several nations into one of the first organized Native American resistance movements, fighting the United States in 1811 in Tecumseh's War. In the Southeast, the Cherokee Nation was technically a separate country, as declared by a signed treaty with the United States. The State of Georgia, however, began to pass laws in 1828 abolishing the Cherokee independence, seized Cherokee land, and sold it off to white Georgians. In 1831 Cherokee leader John Ross attempted to fight back through the US court system, asking the Supreme Court to intervene and stop the land theft.

The Supreme Court sided with the Cherokee, but President Andrew Jackson refused to honor its decision. Ross then gathered sixteen thousand signatures on a petition to protest. It was no use. In 1838 the Cherokee were expelled from their land. Newly elected president Martin Van Buren ordered the US Army to round them up, forcing them to march 1,000 miles (1,609 km) on what became known as the Trail of Tears to a new home in the future state of Oklahoma. Up to five thousand Cherokee died making the trek, including Ross's wife, Quatie Ross. When they arrived, the Cherokee fought back by killing some of the people responsible for the march.

The Supreme Court sided with the Cherokee, but President Andrew Jackson refused to honor its decision.

SLAVE REBELLIONS

African slaves in the early days of North American colonization had few choices against their cruel and often abusive masters. Their options for rebellion included violence or personal acts of resistance, such as refusing to work, both of which could mean terrible punishment.

During the 1739 Stono Rebellion, twenty slaves—many of whom had been warriors in their home country of Angola—raided a store in South Carolina, killing the white owners and placing their heads on the front steps. The slaves then set out on a march toward Saint Augustine, Florida, then a Spanish territory where they would legally be free. As the march grew to more than one hundred slaves, they burned homes and killed more people along the way. They paraded down King's Highway, shouting "*lukango,*" or "liberty," in the Kikongo language, a foreshadowing of the American Revolution to come. The rebellions, crushed by colonial forces after a week, inspired many smaller uprisings.

Nat Turner's Rebellion of 1831 was driven by religious visions of freedom experienced by Turner, a Virginia slave. Along with seventy armed slaves and free Black men, he killed his master's family and attacked more than a dozen homes. More than fifty white slave owners were killed in Turner's uprising. When he was caught and hanged, local slave owners were so angry that they beheaded Turner as a warning to other would-be rebels, and handed out parts of his body as souvenirs.

Not all resistance against slavery was violent or led by slaves themselves. Abolitionists, or people who fought for laws against slavery, staged conferences and speaking tours intended to convince their neighbors to vote for politicians with antislavery platforms. Some, including Henry David Thoreau, refused to pay taxes while the government supported slavery. Others boycotted cotton and other products from southern slave states. Some activists defied the law by harboring escaped slaves or helped them to freedom through a secret system called the Underground Railroad.

Nat Turner led a slave uprising that killed more than fifty slave owners before he was caught and punished by death.

Some white abolitionists turned to violence as well. In 1859 John Brown raided the small town of Harper's Ferry, Virginia, to spark a massive slave uprising to end slavery. Brown intended to seize weapons from a federal arsenal and distribute them to slaves who would fight for their freedom. He and a band of twenty-two men took over the arsenal, but before they could give out any weapons, a company of marines captured him and he was sentenced to death. Brown's raid and other such guerilla attacks became a central issue of the 1860 presidential election, in which Abraham Lincoln became president. The Civil War (1861–1865) would erupt one year later. The war ended legal slavery in the United States.

OTHER UPRISINGS

Besides racism and civil rights, other themes that occupy modern protesters were also present in the past. In Massachusetts in 1787, poor farmers rose up against what they saw as economic exploitation by banks and corrupt politicians, whose policies of personal enrichment after the Revolutionary War (1775–1783) led to inflation and foreclosure of their farms. During Shays' Rebellion, named after a farmhand who led the uprising, a group of farmers attempted to seize weapons and overthrow the government. The United States was so new at the time that it didn't

RIDING THE UNDERGROUND RAILROAD

One of the most effective ways to protest against slavery, if you were a slave, was to disappear. The Fugitive Slave Acts of 1793 and 1850 declared that escaped slaves could be seized and forcibly returned to their masters. Defying these laws and gaining freedom was an ultimate act of resistance. But how did they escape?

The Underground Railroad, a secret network of safe houses and hidden paths, helped escaped slaves reach freedom in Canada through fourteen northern US states. It wasn't actually a railroad, and it wasn't always underground—though there were some tunnels. But the system, created by both former slaves and white abolitionists, was treated symbolically like a railway. The escape routes were called *lines*, stopping places were *stations*, guides and helpers were *conductors*, and slaves were known as *freight* or *packages*.

Over its several decades of existence, conductors, such as Quaker leader Thomas Garrett and former slave Harriet Tubman, helped between forty thousand and one hundred thousand slaves to freedom. Tales of narrow escapes and daring heroism from the railroad fueled the abolition movement in the North that eventually helped end slavery.

even have money for an army to hold back the rebels, so independent armed groups, or *militias*, stepped in to stop them.

The Whiskey Rebellion of 1794 occurred when Pennsylvania farmers who made their own whiskey protested a tax on liquor by destroying the home of a tax collector. The rebellion against the tax spread throughout the young country and threatened to tear it apart. President George Washington sent in the new US Army, which peacefully defused the situation. The fledgling government was growing, and this event showed it could successfully manage a crisis.

Religious intolerance and anti-immigrant bias fueled the Know-Nothing riots in various cities around the country from 1844 to 1858. The nativist American Know Nothing Party was an anti-Catholic, xenophobic political party. It whipped up hysteria that immigrants were committing voter fraud and sent in criminal gangs called the Plug Uglies and the Rip Raps to disrupt voting during local elections, causing riots and occupying government buildings.

The New York draft riots of 1863 started as a protest by working-class white men against being forced to fight in the Civil War (not everyone in the North was against slavery) but escalated into some of the bloodiest rioting in US history, targeting Black men and killing hundreds.

Harriet Tubman was born into slavery. After escaping north with her brothers, she returned south many times to help other enslaved people resist the unfair system of slavery.

CHAPTER 2

CHUCKING TEA FOR LIBERTY

BOSTON TEA PARTY, 1773

THE DESTRUCTION OF TEA AT BOSTON HARBOR

This 1846 lithograph by artist Nathaniel Currier shows the Sons of Liberty rebelling against Britain at Boston Harbor in 1773.

American colonists protest British policies with an act of destruction that helps spark a revolution.

On the chilly, rainy evening of December 16, 1773, about seven thousand people—almost half the population of Boston at the time—gathered around the city's Old South Meeting House. They were about to initiate one of the most iconic acts of rebellion in history.

Led by Samuel Adams, the mass meeting had convened to address what many participants considered a grave injustice. The British government was unfairly taxing residents of the American colonies to pay for the ongoing French and Indian War (1754–1763). Worse, there was little the colonists could legally do about it. Because they were subjects of the British Empire, they had no voice in the British government. The phrase "no taxation without representation" had become a slogan among those who resented British rule and longed for independence.

Of particular urgency was a large shipment of tea. Three ships—the *Dartmouth*, the *Eleanor*, and the *Beaver*—sat at Griffin's Wharf in Boston, loaded with wooden cases of tea from the British East India Tea Company. On May 10, 1773, the British government had passed the Tea Act. The act granted the well-connected East India Tea Company a monopoly on importing tea, by charging colonist-run companies a steep tax. This angered the colonists. Conservative business owners and radical activists such as the secret revolutionary organization the Sons of Liberty, led by Adams, joined together to resist the unfair advantage. They refused to allow the tea to be unloaded, wanting to send the shipment back to England.

Tempers in the colonies were already flaring over British overreach. The Stamp Act of 1765 taxed almost every piece of printed paper the colonists used. In 1770 the city had seen the Boston Massacre, during which British soldiers fired into a crowd of rioting colonists, killing five.

Recent protests against the East India Tea Company monopoly throughout the colonies had been successful. Tea imports in New York and Philadelphia had been turned back or left rotting on the docks. But Massachusetts governor Thomas Hutchinson, a British appointee, would not allow the ships to be sent back to Britain. Hutchinson supported the tax—and his sons were involved in the business that imported the tea. Tonight's gathering at the Old South Meeting House would determine what actions to take. When Adams received word that the governor would not turn back the ships, he knew it was time to take on the government directly.

LIBERTY TREES AND REBELLIOUS STRIPES

Who were the Sons of Liberty? The group began as the Loyal Nine, nine men who met in 1765 to plan resistance to the British. Soon the Loyal Nine grew into a larger organization, with members in most of the colonies, who often met at Liberty Trees—large trees (and sometimes human-made poles) in each town, chosen for their prominence. The name Sons of Liberty quickly caught on.

Like many secretive associations before them, the Sons of Liberty kept their identities hidden but still used highly visible symbols to make a statement. They adopted a striking flag of nine vertical red and white stripes. This flag, flown in defiance of the British government, became known as the Rebellious Stripes. After it was outlawed, the Sons of Liberty adopted a flag used by the navy, with thirteen horizontal red and white stripes. This design was later incorporated into the US flag we use today.

THE POWER OF PAMPHLETS

It's hard to get word out about your revolution when you have to remain anonymous and the government is watching over the press. In an age long before social media, protesters and revolutionaries secretly printed and passed by hand pamphlets and flyers full of ideas and experiences. In the run-up to the Revolutionary War, famous pamphlets including Thomas Paine's "Common Sense" and John Dickinson's "Letters from a Farmer in Pennsylvania" laid out the case for the colonies' independence from Britain. That they were published anonymously and passed along in person helped readers relate to the ideas and feel inspired to share their own. This built momentum for the long fight against the British that lay ahead.

Launching crates of tea into Boston Harbor helped launch the Sons of Liberty into history books.

THE TEA PARTY

About one hundred members of the Sons of Liberty left for the dock where the ships were moored, planning to make a statement the British could not ignore.

Many of them changed into clothing that resembled that worn by Native Mohawk people. The Sons of Liberty smeared one another's faces with soot and red ochre, threw on ragged clothes and blankets, decorated themselves with feathers, and grabbed small hatchets that resembled tomahawks. They wanted to disguise themselves because what they were about to do could get them arrested and sued. They also may have chosen to dress as indigenous people to symbolically show they were more "American" than British. (The Mohawks themselves resisted the colonists and later sided with the British during the Revolutionary War.)

This illustration, published in a Philadelphia newspaper in 1765, portrayed the wax seal required by Britain's Stamp Act as a death head.

At 7 p.m., the Sons of Liberty boarded the three ships and ransacked them for three hours, throwing 342 chests of tea into Boston Harbor. They split as many cases as they could with their hatchets to ruin the tea. The men returned the next morning in small boats to destroy any intact cases still floating on the harbor.

The protest shocked the British, and even American leaders such as Benjamin Franklin insisted that the tea should be paid for. The British government soon passed what became known as the Intolerable Acts, designed to punish the Massachusetts colonists for their defiance. These acts closed the Boston port altogether, severely limited town meetings, and brought Massachusetts more directly under British control. All of these events inspired even more colonists to resist British rule and led to the Revolutionary War.

Despite the backlash from the British, Adams publicly defended the colonists' actions, using "the destruction of the tea" (it was not called the Boston Tea Party until much later) to promote the idea of principled protest, even if it was destructive, to establish American colonists' rights.

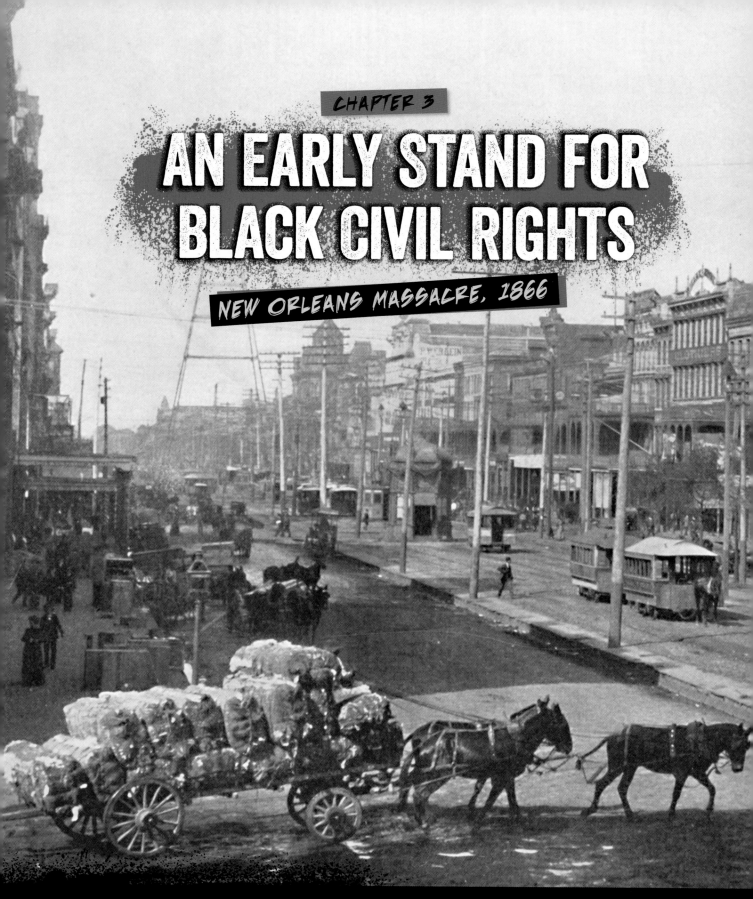

CHAPTER 3

AN EARLY STAND FOR BLACK CIVIL RIGHTS

NEW ORLEANS MASSACRE, 1866

The Civil War ends, but hope for Black equality is crushed after a joyful parade in New Orleans.

How did Black people establish their rights after slavery was abolished in 1865? What happened in 1866 in New Orleans shows the steep challenges faced by former slaves and other Black citizens.

During the Civil War (1861–1865), the bustling Louisiana city of New Orleans was unique. Founded by France and briefly ruled by Spain, it possessed a more diverse culture than much of the rest of the Confederate South. Residents included freed slaves from the Caribbean islands and free people of color, who were of mixed African and European ancestry. Still, New Orleans had relied on slavery for its growth as a major port city, despite its multicultural population and complex social customs.

In 1862, after some fierce battles, the Union had won the city, and Major General Benjamin Franklin Butler and his troops occupied it with little resistance. Butler was a harsh man who liked to start arguments, but he was also a smart politician who found ways to keep the people of New Orleans on his side. While he ruled the city under martial law, he gave food taken from the Confederate army to poor people and employed many of them to help clean up the city. Butler also recruited Black soldiers to the Corps d'Afrique, three military units with Black officers.

But after the war and slavery ended, Butler left and the former mayor of New Orleans, John T. Monroe, was reelected. The city was divided. Almost half of the white people who lived there had fought for the Confederacy and nearly half of the Black people had fought for the Union. That made the atmosphere of the city tense. And Monroe, who had supported the Confederacy, oversaw the enforcement of black codes, or laws that restricted Black people's freedom. White lawmakers still did not allow black people to vote, despite many of them being educated and owning property.

THE MASSACRE

In 1866 the Republican Party wanted to extend voting rights to Black men, as well as repeal the black codes. However, those in power adopted even stricter black code measures, including fines for swearing, loitering, and general disobedience. A group calling themselves Radical Republicans reconvened the state convention in New Orleans, giving Black people and their allies hope for more equality. Local Democrats and former Confederate soldiers, however, believed the convention was illegal and considered it a way for Republicans to increase their power.

An Early Stand for Black Civil Rights

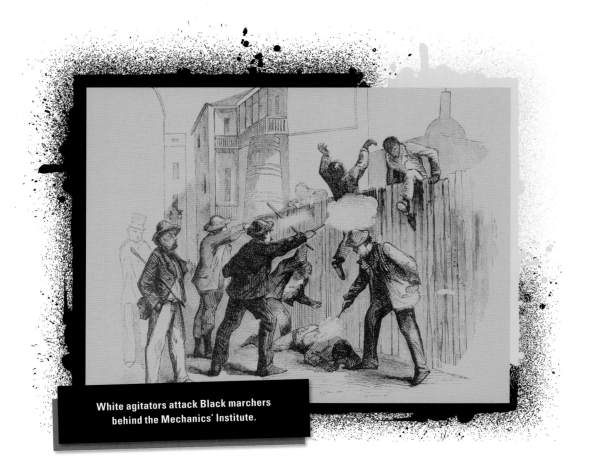

White agitators attack Black marchers behind the Mechanics' Institute.

Three days before the convention, Black war veterans and other supporters gathered on the steps of the Mechanics' Institute, where the state convention was to be held. There, they were thrilled to hear activist speakers, such as the former governor of Louisiana, encourage them to stand up for their rights. They decided to have a parade to support the convention.

On July 30, a jubilant procession of about one hundred Black men began to march toward the Mechanics' Institute from the traditionally Black neighborhood Faubourg Marigny. They waved flags and marched to a brass band. Supporters including women and children lined the streets and cheered, encouraged by the dream of interracial equality.

Soon after the parade started, however, white attackers began verbally and physically assaulting the marchers. The attackers fired shots and a brief battle broke out, but the parade continued toward the institute.

Once they reached the entrance, the marchers faced greater violence. A mob of white supremacists carried out a premeditated attack. Fire sirens went off, signaling the police, mostly former Confederate soldiers sent by the mayor, and armed firefighters to attack the parade. The marchers fought back as best they could and many took refuge in the institute, but their attackers overwhelmed them, beating them with clubs, stabbing them, and shooting them. Assailants bashed marchers' heads with bricks and threw bodies from windows. Men who tried to surrender were killed.

Fifty people died, and dozens more were injured. By the time federal troops arrived—too late to help—they found absolute chaos. The area was full of bodies bleeding on the ground and gun smoke in the air. The incident became a national scandal, known as the New Orleans Massacre, or the New Orleans Race Riots.

Ironically, the outrage the massacre caused (along with that of related violent racial events in several other cities) actually helped the Republican cause throughout the country. This anger contributed to the passing of the Fourteenth Amendment in 1868, granting citizenship to former slaves, and the Fifteenth Amendment in 1870, granting Black people the right to vote.

The parade and the attackers at the New Orleans Massacre

THE TWO-PARTY SWITCH

Reading about US political history can be confusing, because our two main parties, the Democrats and the Republicans, switched roles in the middle of the twentieth century. Before this, the Republicans were the party of Lincoln—against slavery, based in the North, and generally liberal in encouraging Black men to run for office. Meanwhile, the Democrats held power in southern states and were known for discriminatory policies, a conservative yearning for a smaller federal government that gave more power to individual states, and a mostly white base.

The parties began to switch philosophies during the Great Depression, when Democratic president Franklin Delano Roosevelt's New Deal economic policies, seen as very liberal, were embraced by struggling poor white people and people of color. In the 1960s, Democratic president John F. Kennedy expanded outreach to liberals, and Democratic president Lyndon Johnson signed the Civil Rights Act of 1964, a landmark of liberal policy. In response, conservatives fled the Democratic Party in droves, and the Republican Party began supporting conservative presidential candidates Richard Nixon and Barry Goldwater.

By the late 1970s, the transformation of the Democrats into mostly liberals and Republicans into mostly conservatives was complete, cemented by the election of conservative Republican president Ronald Reagan in 1980.

An Early Stand for Black Civil Rights

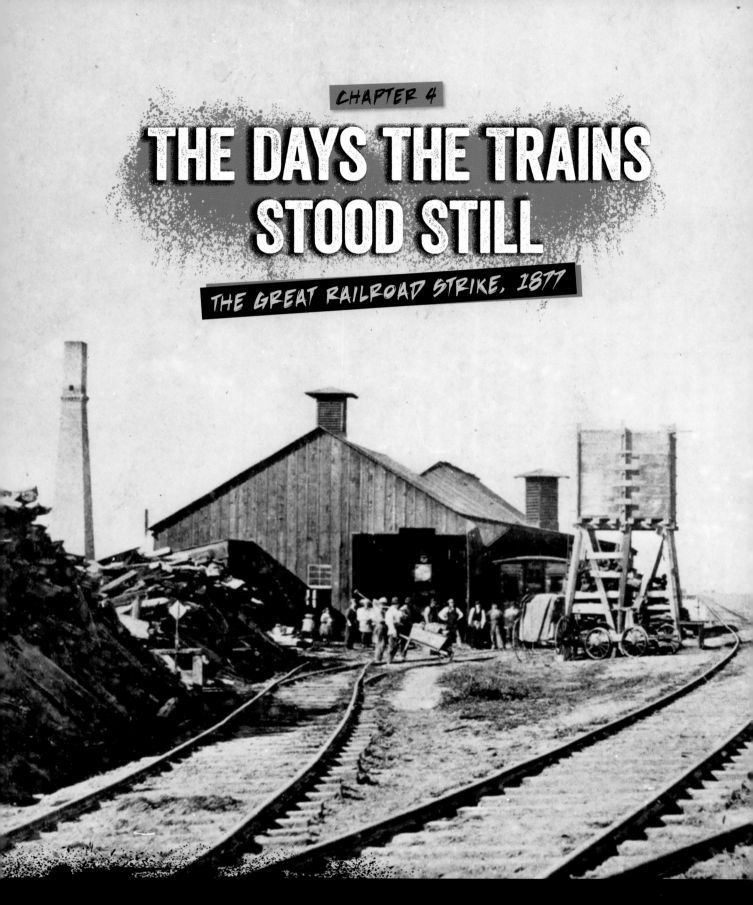

CHAPTER 4

THE DAYS THE TRAINS STOOD STILL

THE GREAT RAILROAD STRIKE, 1877

Alameda Terminal in what is now San Francisco, California, shown here in 1869, was the Pacific coast endpoint of the Transcontinental Railroad

Workers rebel against railroad owners to protest long hours, low pay, and dangerous working conditions.

The railroad business was booming after the Civil War, offering plenty of work for former soldiers and recent immigrants. Workers laid more than 35,000 miles (56,327 km) of new track between 1866 and 1873, connecting more cities than ever. The first transcontinental railroad, completed in 1869, stretched from the Atlantic coast to the Pacific coast.

Conditions, however, were tough. There were no eight-hour workday limits, weekends off, minimum wage, or guaranteed breaks. Jobs rarely had safety requirements, and employers could fire workers at any time. Few trade union organizations existed to empower workers, and the five-day workweek wasn't instituted until 1908 in the United States.

The late nineteenth century was the age of robber barons, or company owners and managers who became rich by not sharing the wealth of their industries with the workers who helped create it. And in 1873, an economic depression gripped the global economy and lasted for years. Tens of thousands of people lost their jobs, wages were cut, and thousands of companies collapsed. Soon railroad workers had to take even more pay cuts and work longer hours. People looking for work, including recent immigrants, newly freed slaves, and people from the country moving to big cities in search of jobs, had to compete with one another. The scene was set for an explosion of working-class protest.

THE STRIKE

On July 16, 1877, employees of the Baltimore and Ohio Railroad rebelled at the announcement of a 10 percent pay cut—the second in eight months. They shut down the station in Martinsburg, West Virginia, and stranded about six hundred trains, demanding their pay be restored. When police and the state militia could not free the trains or disperse the supportive crowds that had gathered, the West Virginia governor called in federal troops.

The troops used force to get the trains running again, but news of the strike had already spread and inspired similar actions along the railways. Soon strikers had halted trains from the East Coast to California.

In Reading, Pennsylvania, workers held mass marches, burned down a railroad bridge, and blocked trains. In East Saint Louis, Illinois, strikers halted all railroad traffic and took over the entire city for a week. In Chicago, coal miners joined railroad workers in a mass strike.

In Philadelphia, strikers fought with the armed state militia and burned much of downtown. Local and state authorities tried to put down each protest, but public sentiment was often on the side of the strikers.

The worst of the violence happened in Pittsburgh, Pennsylvania, where members of the local militia stabbed and shot at strikers who were throwing rocks, killing twenty. This further enraged the strikers, who forced the militiamen into a railroad roundhouse and set fire to several buildings. The next day, the militiamen shot their way out of the roundhouse, killing twenty more strikers.

The workers' determination was strengthened by the harsh attitude of the railroad owners. Thomas Alexander

Chinese railroad workers near Clark Fork River in western Montana

STRIKE IN THE MOUNTAINS

As railroads expanded into the West, where miners were digging out millions of dollars' worth of gold, they created new opportunities for immigrant workers. Laborers from China streamed into California to help lay tracks that would connect "gold country" to the industries and banks of the East. Chinese workers faced racism and extreme working conditions as they tunneled through the snow-capped Sierra Nevada to lay the tracks, in what was then the largest engineering project in the history of the country.

In 1867 they laid down their tools and refused to work any farther, taking a stand against long workdays and wages of one-third as much as white workers. The strike lasted eight days. The Central Pacific Railroad, their employer, dealt with the strikers by choking off the workers' food supplies and transportation, freezing them in the mountains. While the strike failed to change conditions, it was the biggest such labor action of the time, and it helped change the stereotype among white workers of Chinese people as quiet and obedient.

Scott, president of the Pennsylvania Railroad, said the strikers should be given "a rifle diet for a few days and see how they like that kind of bread."

President Rutherford B. Hayes sent armed federal troops to overwhelm the strikers, and one by one, each protest petered out. The strike lasted forty-five days and did an estimated $5 to $10 million in damages. One hundred people were killed, and many workers were fired.

Some historians believe the Great Railway Strike helped spark the union movement in the United States. Later strikes—such as the 1894 Pullman Strike (which gave rise to Labor Day) and the Great Railroad Strike of 1922—were more organized and workers were able to negotiate with the railroad companies.

A Chinese railroad worker camp in Nevada

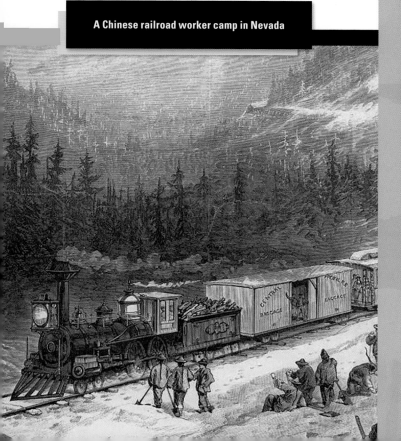

A BOMB GOES OFF

Chicago experienced a building boom after the Great Chicago Fire blazed through the city in 1871. Builders, carpenters, road workers, and food suppliers flooded in to reconstruct the giant city. Workers formed early unions and staged strikes for better working conditions, assisted by political groups, including Socialists, Communists, and anarchists. Police and government figures closely aligned with corporations, and owners considered these groups a threat.

In 1886, as part of a nationwide campaign for an eight-hour workday, tens of thousands of people filled Chicago's Michigan Avenue. They chanted slogans, such as "Eight hours for work, eight hours for rest, eight hours for what we will!" and "Shorten the hours, increase the pay." Afterward, a rally in Haymarket Square to protest police violence itself turned violent when someone threw a bomb near the speakers' platform. Police shot randomly into the crowd, and in the chaos, eleven people were killed.

Although the bomber was never identified, the Haymarket Riot was immediately used as propaganda against the young labor movement. Chicago and other cities across the country declared martial law. Radical newspapers were shut down, meeting halls and private homes were raided, and hundreds were arrested. Because many who led the labor movement were immigrants, the media went into an anti-immigrant frenzy and helped turn popular sentiment against labor organizers. Prominent members of the anarchist movement, which believed that government authority was harmful to free societies, were rounded up and arrested. Eight of them were convicted and seven sentenced to death.

CHAPTER 5

A GRAND PARADE FOR WOMEN'S VOTING RIGHTS

THE WOMAN SUFFRAGE PROCESSION, 1913

About eight thousand activists made their opinions on women's voting rights known at the 1913 Woman Suffrage Procession.

A dazzling spectacle with a serious purpose fills the streets of Washington, DC.

The US Constitution once barred women from voting in national elections, but by the middle of the nineteenth century, a growing movement was calling for women's suffrage, or voting rights. The 1848 Seneca Falls Convention in New York drew three hundred women and men who sought equal civil, social, and religious treatment for women and, as organizer Elizabeth Cady Stanton put it, "to declare our right to be free as man is free."

Other gatherings and actions followed, including annual women's rights conventions from 1850 to 1861. In 1851 Black women's rights crusader Sojourner Truth delivered her famous speech "Ain't I a Woman" at an Ohio women's rights convention. Susan B. Anthony formed the American Equal Rights Association in 1866 and was arrested for voting in 1872.

After the Civil War, the Fourteenth Amendment defined voters as male (the first time that word appeared in the Constitution) and the Fifteenth Amendment extended the right to vote to Black men but not to women. Some states allowed women to vote, usually if they owned property. A women's suffrage amendment was introduced to Congress in 1878, but it was defeated two to one.

THE PROCESSION

In 1913 women were still not legally able to vote in federal elections. Activists believed something big was needed to grab the public's attention. The National American Woman Suffrage Association decided to hold a grand parade in Washington, DC, full of symbolism and pageantry, called the Woman Suffrage Procession. Organizers intended to draw together women's rights activists from around the country to "march in a spirit of protest against the present political organization of society, from which women are excluded."

Organized by activists Alice Paul and Lucy Burns, who had just returned from working with the radical wing of the British suffragette movement, the parade was a big deal for its time. It included several thousand marchers, twenty floats, nine bands, and four mounted brigades—all led by Socialist lawyer and labor union activist Inez Milholland, dressed as a warrior in a cape and helmet, on her own white horse, Gray Dawn. (Typically for the time, the press named her the most beautiful suffragette, which she disliked.)

Highlighting how far the United States was lagging behind, the front of the procession featured representatives of countries that had already granted women the right to vote. A "pioneers" contingent, showcasing women who had fought for suffrage for decades, followed.

Then came women of all occupations wearing their work clothing—nurses, farmers, teachers, pharmacists, librarians, and college women in academic gowns. The parade featured other colorful costumes, a marching homemakers' contingent, representatives from individual states, participants waving large "Votes for Women" flags, and dramatic depictions of the Roman goddess Minerva and other mythological representations of female wisdom and liberty.

The procession was timed to take place the day before Woodrow Wilson's presidential inauguration, when the city was filled with visitors to witness the ceremony. Hundreds of spectators, mostly men, swarmed to the parade, straining for a glimpse of its novelty. But some also heckled, shoved, and tripped participants, overwhelming the parade so much that the National Guards of Massachusetts and Pennsylvania stepped in to help the marchers. A human chain of male students from Maryland Agricultural College protected the procession so it could reach its destination.

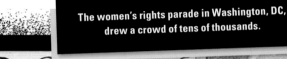

The women's rights parade in Washington, DC, drew a crowd of tens of thousands.

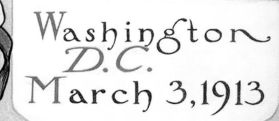

Official Program WOMAN SUFFRAGE Procession

Washington D.C. March 3, 1913

The procession, considered one of the great successes of the women's rights movement, included internal controversy. Before the Civil War, the fight for suffrage had grown out of the fight against slavery. After the Civil War, however, when many women in the South came to prominence in the movement, it became more segregated. In early discussions of the Woman Suffrage Procession, some suffrage leaders wanted to bar Black women from participating. Eventually, suffrage leaders slated them to march at the end, after a contingent of male supporters. (Some Black women marched with white contingents anyway.)

Because it encountered so much trouble and had so many interesting and photogenic elements, the procession attracted national media attention, amplifying its cause. Senate hearings about the mistreatment of participants, which caused a wave of public outrage, resulted in the dismissal of the DC police superintendent and brought the women's rights issue into the mainstream political sphere. Historians credit the parade with helping to build the momentum that led to the Nineteenth Amendment, which prohibits the government from denying the right to vote based on sex.

GIANTS OF THE EARLY WOMEN'S MOVEMENT

Alice Paul (1885–1977) was a main organizer of the Woman Suffrage Procession and many other actions for women's rights. After the Nineteenth Amendment passed in 1920, Paul went on to lead the National Woman's Party, which fought for an equal rights amendment to the Constitution that would protect women from discrimination. Lucy Burns (1879–1966) was a close friend of Paul, organizing the procession and the National Woman's Party with her. Burns was jailed several times, put in solitary confinement, and tortured for her women's rights protests. From jail she led hunger strikes and helped define the rights of political prisoners with her writing and activism.

Susan B. Anthony (1820–1906) is probably the most well-known—and one of the earliest—of women's rights activists. At a time when women were taught to stay quiet, she campaigned for the expansion of women's property rights and an end to slavery, as well as women's suffrage. Philosopher and activist Elizabeth Cady Stanton (1815–1902) was the first president of the National American Woman Suffrage Association, and along with fellow abolitionist and advocate Lucretia Mott (1793–1880) organized the 1848 women's rights convention in Seneca Falls. Ida B. Wells (1862–1931) was a trailblazing journalist who reported on anti-Black violence and discrimination. During the Woman Suffrage Procession, organizers first asked her not to march and then to march at the back of the parade. Wells resisted and defiantly marched near the front.

A Grand Parade for Women's Voting Rights

A RALLY TO INSPIRE FEAR

CHAPTER 6

THE KU KLUX KLAN, 1925

This 1920s ceremony initiated the kneeling man into the growing Ku Klux Klan.

White-hooded figures descend on Washington, DC, with a racist, anti-immigrant agenda.

Protests sometimes take the form of rallies to show strength and support a cause or idea. But what if the goal is to terrify others?

The First Amendment guarantees the right to peaceable assembly. Major court cases over the years have interpreted this to mean that the freedom to hold a protest or rally "does not provide the right to conduct an assembly at which there is a clear and present danger of riot, disorder . . . or other immediate threat to public safety," according to the Law Library of Congress.

At the beginning of the twentieth century, that interpretation was still being defined. Even now, a rally may have a disagreeable or even terrible idea behind it, but it can go forward as long as courts and police consider it legal.

The Ku Klux Klan is a white supremacist hate group that uses terror tactics to oppress racial and religious minorities. It arose during the Civil War out of fear that freed slaves would gain too much power. The Klan attacked Black leaders and citizens and scared many out of participating in government or living in certain areas—but the group died out in the 1870s. However, in the first two decades of the twentieth century, when many people were moving to the United States to escape war and poverty, Klan members resurrected the group to protest immigration laws, attack Catholic and Jewish immigrants, and keep Black people segregated from the rest of society.

This version of the Ku Klux Klan used highly visual techniques, such as wearing white hoods and robes, burning crosses, hanging people from trees (or lynching), and holding mass rallies. They knew the power of an image to instill terror. Because so many of its members were police officers, lawyers, business owners, and members of the government, the Klan got away with most of its actions. In some communities, people even celebrated it as a kind of law enforcement agency.

THE RALLY

In 1925 the Ku Klux Klan was at the height of its popularity. Four million people were members of the organization. Its status had risen because of backlash against waves of immigration after World War I (1914–1918), and the group supported the Immigration Act of 1924, which severely restricted the number of people who could move to the United States.

Calling its massive annual gathering a klonvocation, the Klan had marched in previous years through Washington, DC, which was a highly segregated city, with white people living in some neighborhoods and Black people in others.

A Rally to Inspire Fear

The huge numbers of Klan members in the 1920s was representative of the country's high levels of segregation and racist beliefs.

The Ku Klux Klan march on August 8, 1925, down Pennsylvania Avenue was the largest to date. Participants from across the country filled eighteen trains and took over several DC hotels. While there was no official statement of purpose for the march, its fearsome appearance was a show of strength, as well as a threat to people of color and others to stay in their place.

An estimated fifteen to thirty thousand participants, most wearing hoods and robes, paraded in formations fourteen rows deep with twenty-two people in each row, giving the appearance of a military march. They formed giant human crosses and other geometrical shapes that fascinated tens of thousands of spectators and the media. The marchers, including a women's contingent, hoisted banners identifying where they had traveled from to show how pervasive the organization was. Because it was illegal to march with masks on, many Klan members adjusted their hoods to show their faces. This was unusual, since normally they remained anonymous to escape identification.

"Phantom-like hosts of the Ku Klux Klan spread their white robes over the most historic thoroughfare yesterday in one of the greatest demonstrations this city has ever known," read the *Washington Post*'s gushing account of the march. (Many members of the media were also members of the Ku Klux Klan.)

Also, according to the *Washington Post*, "That evening 75,000 people witnessed—many watching from roadsides and their backyards—the burning of an electrically lit 80-foot [24 m] cross at the Arlington Park horse grounds."

The day of the march was hot—the Ku Klux Klan even brought its own ambulances to remove people who passed out from the heat. But a huge rainstorm interrupted the march and rally. L. A. Mueller, the Grand Kleagle (leader) of the District of Columbia, implored people not to leave due to the rains. "It will not rain. . . . Never yet has God poured rain on a Klan assembly!" he told the marchers. But the rains came, and the rally quickly died out.

The Ku Klux Klan came back to march the next year, but fewer than half the people from 1925 showed up. Five years later, the Ku Klux Klan's membership had dwindled to forty-five thousand.

HATE IN THE STREETS

Protests can be expressions of hope and inclusion. They can also be statements of hatred or anger. From the Know Nothing riots of 1844 (see chapter 1) through the Unite the Right rally of 2017 (see chapter 33), groups have taken to the streets to howl against immigrants, Jews, Black people, and just about every other minority group. Nazi supporters held a huge rally in New York City's Madison Square Garden in 1939, and neo-Nazis marched through a Detroit LGBTQ Pride celebration in 2019.

Like other organized protests, these are protected by the First Amendment's guarantee of free speech and peaceable assembly. The right of hate groups to hold demonstrations was upheld by the Supreme Court in 1977, when the Village of Skokie, Illinois, tried to prevent a neo-Nazi rally.

Many citizens of Skokie were Jewish—some were Holocaust survivors—and were horrified at the thought of neo-Nazis marching through their town. The local government attempted to block the rally by imposing huge permit fees and banning the wearing of uniforms. The Supreme Court said this was unconstitutional. So instead, the residents of Skokie came up with an ingenious counterprotest. They erected a Holocaust museum where the rally was supposed to take place, which remains open to this day. (After all the fuss, the neo-Nazis ended up marching in nearby Chicago.)

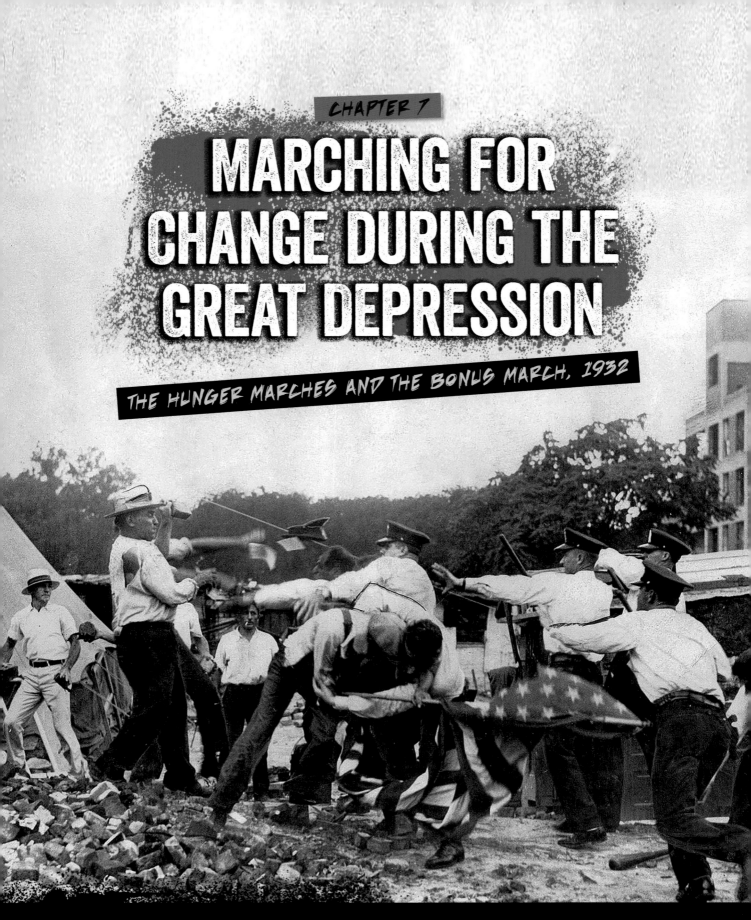

CHAPTER 7

MARCHING FOR CHANGE DURING THE GREAT DEPRESSION

THE HUNGER MARCHES AND THE BONUS MARCH, 1932

Federal government troops remove veteran Bonus March protesters from the streets of Washington, DC.

Poor people and veterans protest government inaction in the face of economic collapse.

Lack of money and a bad economy can lead to protests asking the government for relief. Sometimes the government is directly responsible for the policies that led people to poverty, and protesters hope to change these policies. Other times the government may not be directly responsible, but it can offer programs to help people put food on the table or find jobs. In those cases, protests can spur government officials into action by showing how frustrated people are.

New York's Stock Market Crash of 1929 led to the Great Depression (1929–1942), which affected people around the world. In the United States, around fourteen million people lost their jobs, and huge numbers of people found themselves homeless and impoverished. The Great Depression caused many to question the government's economic and social policies. Unemployed people were looking for jobs or other means of income, while those who had kept their jobs often found their paychecks slashed or their workload increased.

THE HUNGER MARCHES

Year after year, as bills began piling up and options seemed fewer and fewer, people grew angrier. This led to a number of what activists called hunger marches, in which people protested poverty and demanded change. In December 1931 in Washington, DC, the Unemployed Councils of the USA, a Communist group that questioned the system that had led to the Depression and demanded unemployment insurance and money for people to help survive the winter, organized a small march.

A few weeks later, in January 1932, a Catholic priest from Pittsburgh, Father James Renshaw Cox, led a parade of twenty-five thousand unemployed people from Pennsylvania through the streets of Washington, DC, to protest unemployment. Known as Cox's Army, the marchers wanted the government to start a public works program that would create jobs and to raise taxes on the wealthy to pay for it. Cox's Army was the largest demonstration to date in the capital. But instead of listening to their demands, President Herbert Hoover was embarrassed and ordered an investigation into where Cox got money to organize such a huge march.

The most violent hunger march of the time was in Michigan in March 1932, when autoworkers marched through the streets of Detroit to demand that Ford Motor Company end racial discrimination in hiring practices, rehire the unemployed, give workers the right to organize unions to protect their jobs, provide health care for workers and their families, and more. The police and Ford's security guards attacked the marchers, beating them, firing tear gas, and eventually shooting at them with machine guns. Five marchers died, and dozens were injured.

Marching for Change during the Great Depression

Being forced to live in Pittsburgh shanty towns such as this one led the activists of Cox's Army to march on Washington to ask for change.

THE BONUS MARCH

Many US veterans of World War I, which had ended a decade earlier, lost their jobs during the Great Depression. In May 1932, several of them started arriving in Washington, DC, to demand that Congress pay them early for a promised bonus for fighting in the war. Calling themselves the Bonus Expeditionary Forces (later known as the Bonus Army) and led by Walter W. Waters, a former sergeant and cannery worker, the group grew to more than forty-three thousand people, including veterans and their families, who camped out to demand payment.

Like Cox's Army, the Bonus Army embarrassed the government. On July 28, the attorney general ordered the police to remove all the protesters' belongings and kick them off government property. The protesters fought back, and two veterans were killed. Hoover ordered the army in to clear out the protesters. General Douglas MacArthur, the army chief of staff, was enraged and sent soldiers on horseback and tanks to drive out the protesters. He ordered the burning of all of their possessions.

MacArthur thought the Bonus Army wanted to overthrow the government. But as the *Christian Science Monitor* reported at the time, "This was not a revolutionary situation. This was a bunch of people in great distress wanting help. . . . These were simply veterans from World War I who were out of luck, out of money, and wanted to get their bonus—they needed the money at that moment."

The violent handling of the protesters upset voters across the country. Hoover lost the 1932 presidential election in a landslide, and Franklin Roosevelt took office. Although sympathetic to the veterans' cause—he sent his wife, Eleanor, to meet with their leaders—he didn't grant their bonuses early. He did provide for jobs for many of them through a public works program called the Civilian Conservation Corps. But in 1936 he vetoed a bill to pay veterans $2 billion in bonuses. Fortunately for the veterans, Congress overrode the veto and they were paid.

ON THE FRONT LINES

FATHER JAMES RENSHAW COX (1886–1951)

Cox was the Pittsburgh priest who led thousands of unemployed Pennsylvanians to Washington, DC, in 1932 to demand relief. Cox's Army spurred the creation of a political party called the Jobless Party. Cox ran for president in 1932. He later became known as the pastor of the poor because of his involvement with his city's homeless and unemployed.

ELEANOR ROOSEVELT (1884–1962)

Despite her husband's refusal to pay the veterans' bonuses, the new First Lady sympathized with their plight. One afternoon she slipped away from her handlers and forged through the rain and mud to join demonstrating veterans in a long conversation and sing-along. "They looked at me curiously, and one of them asked my name and what I wanted," she recalled later. "When I said I just wanted to see how they were getting on, they asked me to join them."

As one veteran said, "Hoover sent the army, Roosevelt sent his wife." It was Eleanor Roosevelt's first effort as a White House emissary. She soon became known for her activism on behalf of the poor and people of color.

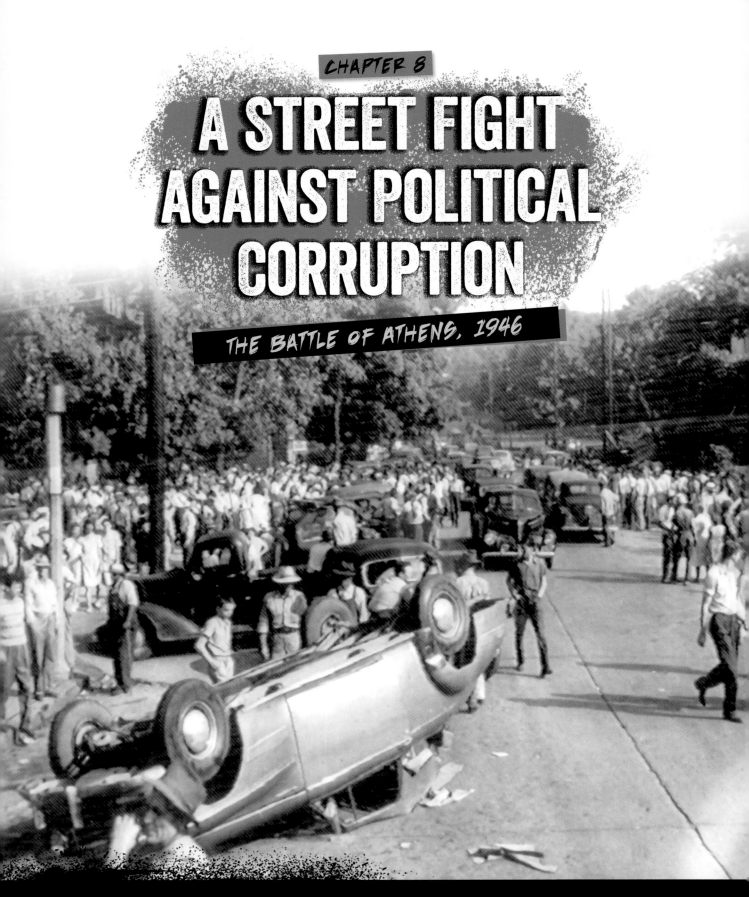

CHAPTER 8

A STREET FIGHT AGAINST POLITICAL CORRUPTION

THE BATTLE OF ATHENS, 1946

Veterans in McMinn County threw sticks of dynamite, among other destructive acts, during a battle with corrupt local government officials.

Veterans take up arms when rigged elections threaten democracy in Tennessee.

Sometimes politicians do sneaky things to win elections. They may change laws, disqualify their opponents, or deny certain people the right to vote. Networks of politicians called *machines* can attempt to make sure only candidates that they approve win elections. This can lead to corruption and fraud, as money begins to disappear and votes don't seem to count. In 1946 war veterans in Tennessee took up arms to defeat this corruption.

People in McMinn County, Tennessee—including the city of Athens—had suspected voter fraud in their area, especially involving their county sheriff, Paul Cantrell. Cantrell was from a wealthy family and was part of a powerful political machine based in Memphis. From 1936 to 1940 he had been elected sheriff three times, and then he was elected state senator in 1942 and 1944.

Shady things were going on. Changes in laws made it easier for Cantrell and his friends to get elected and harder for other people to challenge them. Votes under the names of dead people were recorded. Poll taxes—ways to make people pay to vote—were manipulated to ensure the incumbents won.

Bribery and intimidation ran rampant. The sheriff and his deputies got paid based on the number of arrests they made, so false arrests grew exponentially. They pulled over and ticketed travelers for made-up reasons, earning the area a bad reputation. After Cantrell's election to the state senate, a new sheriff, Pat Mansfield, was elected, and he seemed just as corrupt. Because most of McMinn County's young men were away fighting in World War II (1939–1945), fewer people could challenge deputies when they exerted direct control over public institutions, schools, and the press. Many citizens of McMinn felt things were rigged against them.

When two service members on leave in McMinn were shot and killed, many suspected supporters of the county government were responsible. That's when the rest of McMinn's overseas soldiers realized the extent of what was happening. They became eager to get back home and restore democracy.

THE BATTLE

When the war ended in 1945, more than three thousand men returned from overseas, looking to root out the corruption in McMinn County. At first, they tried to change things democratically. After a secret meeting, five veterans and one civilian decided to run against Cantrell and Mansfield's group in the 1946 election as a GI slate. Later, a large rally of veterans helped whip up

A Street Fight against Political Corruption

enthusiasm for the slate before the election. However, many people still worried that their votes would not count. In an attempt to reassure them, the GIs made their campaign slogan, "Your Vote Will Be Counted as Cast!"

On August 1, 1946, more people turned out to vote than anytime in McMinn's recent history. Mansfield hired two hundred armed deputies to stand watch at the polls and intimidate people into voting his way. The GIs had their own representatives at the polls to make sure the election was fair. As soon as voting started, fights broke out between their observers and the deputies. When one deputy told an Athens man, Tom Gillespie, that he was not allowed to vote and Gillespie tried to vote anyway, he was beaten and shot in the back as he tried to run away. Gillespie later recovered, but the attack ignited tempers. Deputies confiscated ballot boxes, guns were drawn, and a crowd of people ducked behind cars to avoid being shot.

Athens GIs raided local gambling houses to try to stop the corruption in their town. A local looks over the smashed slot machines and punchboards.

When officials began counting the ballots that hadn't been stolen, the GIs were ahead by a three-to-one margin. But the remaining ballot boxes were with deputies at the Athens jail. The GIs had gathered at their campaign headquarters to discuss their next move when two deputies appeared, showed their guns and badges, and commanded the crowd to disperse.

The veterans rioted, fighting back against the deputies' reinforcements and causing two days of chaos in Athens. The veterans threw dynamite bombs, burned cars, and smashed windows. Five deputies were disarmed, beaten, taken outside of town, stripped of their clothing, and told to run back to Georgia where they came from. Veterans armed themselves with almost one hundred thousand rounds of ammunition and stormed the jail. They peppered the walls with gunshots and chased away the deputies, thus retrieving the uncounted ballot boxes.

The real ballot count showed that the GIs had won in a landslide. They restored some order to the county, putting caps on elected officials' salaries to prevent further corruption and changing the way elections were held. Unfortunately, the government soon reverted to its old ways, but returning World War II veterans proved to be a vital political force that influenced the US political landscape for decades.

A LEGACY OF VOTING RIGHTS PROTESTS

When the United States was founded, it was unique in guaranteeing citizens the right to vote—but only certain types of citizens. These white male property owners comprised only 6 percent of the population in 1789. As seen in previous chapters, Black people and women protested for many years for their right to vote. Native Americans could not vote until 1947, unless they joined the military. Chinese, Japanese, Filipino, and Indian people were barred from becoming citizens and, therefore, voting for long periods of US history, until all people of Asian ancestry were granted the right to become citizens in 1952. In many states, convicted felons still can't vote. Before 1971 people had to be twenty-one years old to vote.

Besides restricting the right to vote by identity or status, there were other ways to keep people from voting. Poll taxes required the payment of a fee to register to vote, which kept poor people from voting. Literacy tests restricted voting to the educated. Religious tests and loyalty oaths, which demanded that voters and officeholders belong to certain groups, limited who could run until 1961. Moving polling places, redrawing voting districts, requiring certain types of identification to vote, and making it hard for voters to register can all influence election outcomes. And corrupt politicians and groups have used everything from stealing votes and bribing vote counters to outright violence at the polls to win elections. The elements that ignited the Battle of Athens were not new.

The Voting Rights Act of 1965, signed in response to civil rights movement protests, outlawed discriminatory practices in voting. And when parts of the act were declared unconstitutional by the Supreme Court in 2013, it sparked . . . you guessed it, more protests.

A Street Fight against Political Corruption

CHAPTER 9

ROSA PARKS REFUSES TO GIVE UP HER SEAT

THE MONTGOMERY BUS BOYCOTT, 1955

African Americans showed the country how much power they really had during the bus boycott in Alabama.

The civil rights movement swings into high gear with an iconic protest by a quiet tailor.

After the Civil War, there was a brief hope that Black people would attain equal rights in the United States during Reconstruction. Soon, however, lawmakers passed racist laws throughout the South (and similar laws were often observed in the North). Jim Crow laws, named after a popular stage character who made fun of Black people, restricted access to jobs, housing, education, voting, government services, travel, and much more. Black people were required to use separate bathrooms, go to separate schools, enter through separate doors at many businesses and public spaces, and drink from separate water fountains.

In Montgomery, Alabama, a growing civil rights movement for racial equality protested Jim Crow laws affecting one of the most ordinary daily activities: riding on a bus. By city law, Black people were required to sit at the back of a public bus or to move there if a white person wanted their seat. It was even illegal for a Black person to sit next to a white person. Bus drivers sometimes beat Black people, left them stranded, or harassed Black passengers if they entered through the front door of the bus instead of through the back.

In 1955 there were stirrings of resistance against such restrictions. Black activists and the National Association for the Advancement of Colored People (NAACP) had won some recent court victories against Jim Crow laws. In 1946 the US Supreme Court had ruled that buses that crossed state lines could not be segregated. In the landmark 1954 *Brown v. Board of Education* case, the Supreme Court had declared that segregating schools was unconstitutional.

Activists knew it was just as important to concentrate on changing things at a local level. In March 1955, after fifteen-year-old Claudette Colvin was arrested, handcuffed, and forced off a Montgomery bus when she refused to give up her seat to a white man, activists began to build a case against the system of bus segregation. The NAACP looked for a sympathetic face to focus

> **In March 1955, after fifteen-year-old Claudette Colvin was arrested, handcuffed, and forced off a Montgomery bus when she refused to give up her seat to a white man, activists began to build a case against the system of bus segregation.**

Rosa Parks Refuses to Give Up Her Seat

media attention on the movement. But because Colvin was so young (and pregnant at the time), she was passed over.

Colvin was still a pioneer of civil rights resistance who played a larger role later on, and her arrest inspired others to fight back—particularly her youth council adviser, Rosa Parks.

THE BOYCOTT

Parks had worked as a secretary for the NAACP, helping to bring women's issues into the organization's mission. A quietly dignified, educated forty-two-year-old who worked as a tailor, she was a perfectly relatable person to be the face of a campaign of civil disobedience that could

SITTING DOWN FOR FREEDOM

Inspired by Parks's simple, graceful act of protest and angered by the brutal murder of fourteen-year-old Emmett Till, four close-knit Black freshmen at the North Carolina Agricultural and Technical College wanted to plan an action of their own. Living in the city of Greensboro, the four were forbidden under Jim Crow laws to eat at the same restaurants as white people. They decided to hold a sit-in.

Calmly, dressed in some of their nicest winter clothes, the Greensboro Four entered F. W. Woolworth department store on February 1, 1960. They bought a few items, careful to keep the receipts. Then they sat down at the "whites only" lunch counter and politely ordered some food. The waitstaff refused to serve them, but the men didn't leave. The manager called the police, but they declined to take action because the men were paying customers and were not causing any loud trouble.

The Greensboro Four had cunningly arranged for a friend to tip off the media about their action, and it was all over the papers the next day. For the next five days, the Greensboro Four returned to the lunch counter to sit. Each day their protest grew as students from other colleges joined them. On February 6, the sit-in numbered one thousand people, packing Woolworth's and spilling out into the street. The next week, students in other parts of North Carolina held sit-ins, and soon there were sit-ins at Woolworth's stores in several states. In July, Woolworth's declared that its lunch counters would be integrated.

The sit-in movement was powerful, and by August 1961, more than seventy thousand people had participated in sit-ins around the country. There were also "kneel-ins" at segregated churches, "sleep-ins" at segregated motel lobbies, "swim-ins" at segregated pools, "watch-ins" at segregated movie theaters, and more.

change people's minds about segregation. Her action that set a huge boycott in motion was not planned, however. It happened spontaneously.

On December 1, 1955, Parks was riding a bus home from work. When white people boarded, the driver got up to tell a row of Black people to move so the white people could sit down. Parks recognized him as the same driver who had kicked her off his bus twelve years earlier and driven away without her. "When that white driver stepped back toward us," Parks later told an interviewer, "when he waved his hand and ordered us up and out of our seats, I felt a determination cover my body like a quilt on a winter night."

She scooted over toward the window but refused to move to the "colored section." She was arrested, fingerprinted, imprisoned, and fined fourteen dollars. NAACP president E. D. Nixon bailed her out of jail, Parks appealed the arrest, and the ball was rolling on a major protest.

Parks's spontaneous act of resistance and resulting arrest launched a huge activist movement.

FREEDOM RIDERS

A collective effort can change unjust laws—which was the case with segregation laws in the South. But how do you ensure that the new laws are being enforced? One way is to test them to see what happens. In the summer of 1961, a group of bus riders did just that.

The Supreme Court had ruled that not only was segregating bus seats illegal—segregating bus station restaurants, bathrooms, waiting areas, and other spaces was too. On May 4, thirteen women and men, seven Black and six white, boarded two buses in Washington, DC, headed for New Orleans. These were the first Freedom Riders. They wanted to make sure southern states were following the new laws. The idea for the bus ride had come from a similar ride in 1947 called the Journey of Reconciliation, which had also tested desegregation laws.

The 1961 journey went badly. In South Carolina, Freedom Rider John Lewis (who later became a congressional representative) was attacked when he tried to enter a "whites only" waiting room. In Alabama a mob slashed the tires of one bus, smashed its windows, and grabbed at the riders. Someone threw a firebomb into the bus, and the mob blocked the door so the riders would burn alive. When the riders escaped the flaming bus, they were beaten. The local hospital refused to treat them.

The second bus met a similar fate. At the bus station in Birmingham, members of the Ku Klux Klan and the police attacked riders. They were beaten with baseball bats, bicycle chains, and iron pipes. The riders were determined to continue, but with news of more mobs waiting down the road and bus companies refusing to let them board, the riders took a plane to New Orleans for a civil rights rally.

Their attempt inspired hundreds more Freedom Riders, many of them college students on summer break, to travel through the South. A few years later, the Freedom Summer of 1964 sent more students—many of them part of the Student Nonviolent Coordinating Committee—traveling throughout the South in a massive drive to register Black voters.

That night Nixon and college professor Jo Ann Robinson drew up handbills saying, "If we do not do something to stop these arrests, they will continue. The next time it may be you, or your daughter, or mother." They called for a boycott. Activists handed out thirty-five thousand of these handbills throughout the Black community.

More than forty thousand people boycotted the buses on December 5. They carpooled, took Black-owned taxis, or walked up to 20 miles (32 km) to and from work. The success of the one-day boycott energized the city's Black leaders, including future civil rights movement legends the Reverend Ralph Abernathy and a young minister named Martin Luther King Jr. They started planning something bigger.

There had been a nationwide surge of energy toward civil rights activism in the wake of the tragic murder of Emmett Till earlier that year. Till, a fourteen-year-old boy accused of whistling at a white woman, was kidnapped, beaten, and lynched by white men in Mississippi. In a brave protest, the boy's mother insisted on displaying his body in an open casket so people could see the violence that was happening. Pictures of his funeral published in national magazines had produced outrage. Harnessing the power of that outrage and the enthusiasm of the boycott's participants, King announced that the bus boycott would continue.

For the next 381 days, Black people carpooled, cabbed, hitchhiked, biked, walked, or even rode in horse-drawn carriages to work. The boycott caused huge financial damage to the bus companies that the city used, demonstrating the power and influence of the Black community. The boycott also spurred a backlash. Many people who disagreed with it joined the White Citizens' Council, a bigoted group that attacked the boycotters. The Ku Klux Klan firebombed King's home and Nixon's yard, as well as four black churches. But even when he and eighty-eight other movement leaders were arrested, King urged his followers to stay nonviolent and focused.

Boycott leaders took the case against bus segregation all the way to the Supreme Court. In November 1956, the court affirmed that enforced segregation of Black and white passengers on buses violates the Constitution. This was a huge victory and real momentum for the civil rights movement and King, its young leader.

Rosa Parks Refuses to Give Up Her Seat

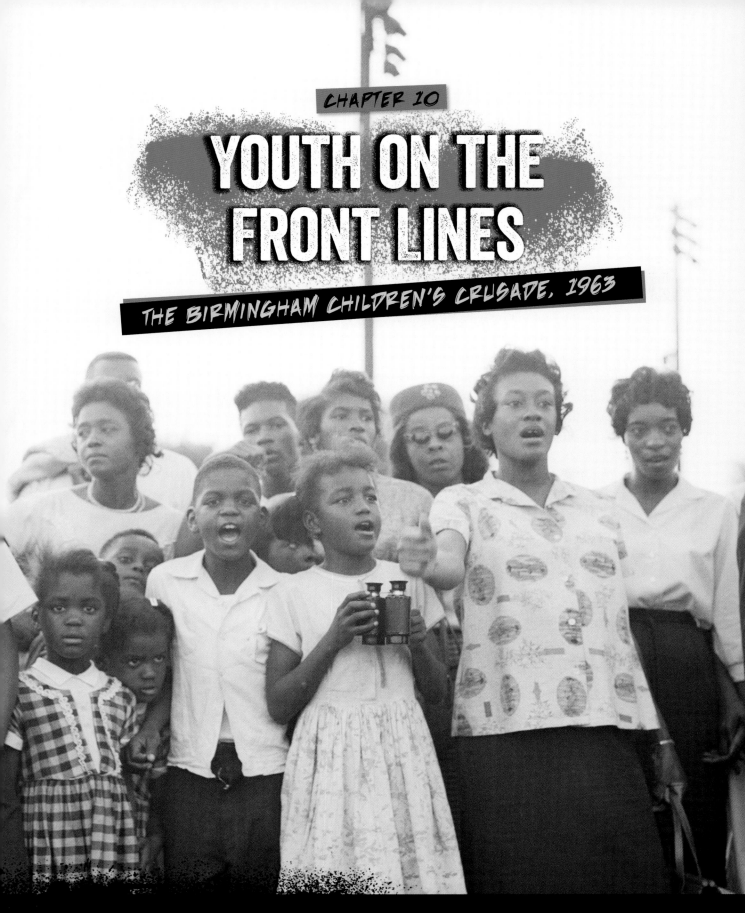

CHAPTER 10

YOUTH ON THE FRONT LINES

THE BIRMINGHAM CHILDREN'S CRUSADE, 1963

Alabama children, some as young as six years old, used their bodies and voices to resist in 1963.

When a campaign for desegregation loses steam, schoolchildren brave violence to protest for their future.

Birmingham, Alabama, was one of the most segregated places in the country in 1963. Backlash against federally ordered school integration in 1954 had inflamed division in the community and emboldened racists. It was normal to see posted signs that said such things as "We Want White Tenants in our White Community" and "Keep Alabama White."

Martin Luther King Jr. visited the city in January 1963 to witness conditions there. His organization, the Southern Christian Leadership Conference, and the local Alabama Christian Movement for Human Rights planned a series of demonstrations—sit-ins, marches, boycotts, direct actions, and more—called the Birmingham campaign. The events were intended to be "a moral witness to give our community a chance to survive," according to the "Birmingham Manifesto," a document written by civil rights leader Fred Shuttlesworth. The campaign launched on April 2, aimed at bringing national attention to Birmingham's situation.

Despite the enthusiasm at the beginning of the campaign, however, it soon fizzled. Money quickly ran out. The city government won an injunction against the protests, so it could order mass arrests—and few workers could afford to lose pay. King was arrested on April 12 and wrote his famous "Letter from a Birmingham Jail," justifying his method of nonviolence.

After King was released on April 20, things looked bleak. The hundreds of volunteers from the beginning of the campaign had dwindled. King's fellow organizer James Bevel came up with an audacious idea. Schoolchildren, eager to help, had been showing up in droves to the special civil rights workshops that were part of the campaign. Why not encourage them to join the protest? The children's march, or Children's Crusade, would use the untapped power of young people who weren't constrained by the jobs and daily responsibilities of their elders. The spectacle of children protesting would also draw media attention to the cause. Reluctantly, King agreed.

THE CAMPAIGN

On May 2, more than a thousand Black elementary, high school, and college students left school and attempted a peaceful march from the 16th Street Baptist Church to City Hall, requesting to speak to the mayor about segregation. The youth, some as young as six years old, sang songs, such as "This Little Light of Mine" and "Ain't Gonna Let Nobody Turn Me Around," as they set off.

The children had been trained in nonviolence. "We were told what to expect when we marched, if we did encounter the police," said participant Carolyn McKinstry, then fourteen. "They might hit you, they might spit on you, they may have dogs and billy clubs. But the only appropriate response, ever, is no response, or a prayerful response."

Police battalions intercepted the march and arrested more than six hundred students. Nevertheless, hundreds more gathered the next day to march. Notoriously bigoted police commissioner Bull Connor and his men were there to meet them. With journalists and photographers from the media present, Connor ordered the Birmingham police and firefighters to use full force to stop the young protesters. They attacked the children with high-pressure fire hoses, set vicious dogs on them, and beat them with clubs. As jails overflowed with children, new arrestees were put in outdoor cages.

Much of this was captured on film and broadcast or printed in newspapers throughout the country, eliciting shock and outrage. The adverse reaction to the images caused Birmingham businesses to lose money and undermined the city government's legitimacy. The dedication of the children reenergized the campaign, and adults joined in. The marches continued for three more days. Robert F. Kennedy, the US attorney general, sent in representatives to pressure city

A few days in, adults joined children in standing up for civil rights in Birmingham.

leaders to negotiate. Spurred by the images and a noticeable change in public perception of the civil rights movement, President John F. Kennedy announced plans for the Civil Rights Act, which passed in 1964 after his assassination.

Still, discrimination was so deeply rooted in Alabama that violent resistance to desegregation, even aimed at children, continued. On September 15, the Ku Klux Klan bombed the 16th Street Baptist Church, killing four little girls.

AT THE FOREFRONT OF A GREAT CHANGE

While the fight for civil rights was a long struggle rooted in the founding of the United States, a new generation of organizers and activists astonished the public with their progress on the issue. "Letter from a Birmingham Jail" cemented the leadership of Martin Luther King Jr. (1929–1968) in the civil rights movement, with its call for justice for all people. His close friend and fellow Christian preacher Ralph Abernathy (1926–1990) collaborated with King to organize the Montgomery Bus Boycott. Abernathy cofounded the Southern Christian Leadership Conference, a crucial civil rights organization, and would later lead the Poor People's Campaign (see chapter 11) after King was assassinated in 1968.

Bayard Rustin (1912–1987) was a civil rights movement mastermind, an early gay rights activist who took care of much of the technical, behind-the-scenes details, such as organizing plans and permits for marches and setting up state-of-the-art sound systems for protests. He organized early Freedom Rides (see chapter 9) and later in life worked to help international refugees. John Lewis (1940–), a Freedom Rider who was beaten in the South, led many protests. He was chairman of the Student Nonviolent Coordinating Committee, part of the huge March on Washington (see chapter 11). He is a US congressional representative from Georgia.

Women were involved too. Dorothy Cotton (1930–2018) was the highest-ranking woman in the Southern Christian Leadership Conference. She organized the Citizen Education Program to teach students and adults about their rights, as well as provide educational opportunities to poor and overlooked Black communities. Diane Nash (1938–) organized lunch counter sit-ins and Freedom Rides. She cofounded the Student Nonviolent Coordinating Committee and worked specifically with young people throughout the movement. Dorothy Height (1912–2010) was a key organizer of the 1963 March on Washington, and as president of the National Council of Negro Women, she helped found the National Women's Political Caucus, which advocates for women running for elected office.

CHAPTER 11

THEY HAD A DREAM

MARCH ON WASHINGTON FOR JOBS AND FREEDOM, 1963

Activists at the 1963 March on Washington had ten demands for their government,
including the topics of desegregation, fair hiring practices, and better pay.

A meticulously planned march and rally becomes the symbol of the civil rights movement.

This highly orchestrated and media-friendly rally for civil rights is one of the most famous demonstrations in US history, along with the protests against the Vietnam War (1957–1975) that would soon follow. Here, Martin Luther King Jr. gave his "I Have a Dream" speech from the Lincoln Memorial and photographers took iconic pictures of Black citizens gathered on the National Mall, peacefully demanding their rights. A key event of the civil rights movement, the rally built on all the nonviolent sit-ins, protests, Freedom Rides, and acts of civil disobedience that had come before. But it was far from the end of the fight for equal rights.

In 1941 labor organizer A. Philip Randolph had called for a march on Washington to bring attention to the government's discriminatory hiring practices, which excluded Black people from jobs in the defense industry during World War II. The prospect of a rally of up to one hundred thousand people criticizing his administration prodded President Franklin Roosevelt to create the Fair Employment Practice Committee, meant to address the inequality. Activists learned that just the *idea* of a large march of Black people could bring about change and saved that knowledge for later use.

After the landmark 1954 *Brown v. Board of Education* ruling by the Supreme Court, which struck down "separate but equal" segregation in public schools and other institutions, two civil rights demonstrations were held at the capital—the 1957 Prayer Pilgrimage for Freedom and the 1958 Youth March for Integrated Schools—to keep the progress of desegregation going.

However, "by 1963, the centennial of the Emancipation Proclamation, most of the goals of these earlier protests still had not been realized. High levels of black unemployment, work that offered most African Americans only minimal wages and poor job mobility, systematic disenfranchisement of many African Americans, and the persistence of racial segregation in the South prompted discussions about a large scale march for political and economic justice," according to the Martin Luther King, Jr. Research and Education Institute.

This inspired the Negro American Labor Council and other large activist organizations to follow Randolph's original protest plan. For this new protest, Randolph himself wrote the letter requesting a permit for a march and gathering. Joining Randolph in sponsoring the march were a diverse group of powerful activist figureheads, including King.

The march and rally took three months to plan. Several more big organizations signed up to participate, and people from all over the country traveled to Washington, DC. Bayard Rustin, a brilliant strategist of nonviolent actions, headed up the planning. He realized that things might quickly get out of control. The march needed to be planned down to the slightest detail to

In 1965 activists in Alabama continued the fight for civil rights with a march from Selma to Montgomery.

ensure that it was effective and that it made a good impression. Rustin considered everything, from the size of the sound system for featured speakers to where the portable toilets should go. He even created an organizing manual that trained parade marshals, detailed logistics, and provided talking points for speaking to the media.

THE MARCH AND RALLY

Rustin had estimated that about 100,000 people would show up, but on August 28, 1963, around 250,000 people—190,000 Black and 60,000 white—came out. President John F. Kennedy, who had just proposed the sweeping Civil Rights Act, was nervous about the crowd. If any trouble occurred in a gathering that large, popular sentiment could turn against his legislation. Since it was the first large demonstration of Black people broadcast on TV, many expected mass arrests and rioting.

But the march was orderly and uplifting, with extended families, church groups and religious congregations, and arts and labor organizations joining together to walk peacefully, singing songs such as "We Shall Overcome" and "Oh Freedom." Marching from the Washington Monument to the Lincoln Memorial, they carried signs that said "We Demand Equality Rights Now" and "Civil Rights Plus Full Employment Equals Freedom."

After the march, crowds gathered on the Mall in a picnic-like atmosphere and listened to songs from famous singers Marian Anderson, Mahalia Jackson, Joan Baez, and Bob Dylan. Dozens of celebrities attended. Speeches given from the Lincoln Memorial laid out the demands of the march, including access to all public accommodations, decent housing, adequate and integrated education, the right to vote for all people, and a higher minimum wage.

The highlight was King's speech, with soaring lines that envisioned a world that didn't judge people by their race but by how they acted. After the march, leaders met with Kennedy to talk about his civil rights legislation.

Although a few glitches occurred—and some people including radical activist Malcolm X complained that the march was too tame, failing to transmit the real anger of Black people at their situation—the march impressed millions of people as it was broadcast around the country, and it was called "a triumph of managed protest."

SELMA: THE MARCH CONTINUES

The March on Washington made King a media star—a status he ingeniously used to continue the momentum of the civil rights movement. Along with other leaders, he focused on local action that would bring attention to discrimination's devastating effects on communities throughout the country. In 1965 King led a five-day, 54-mile (87 km) march from Selma, Alabama, to the state capital, Montgomery, to draw attention to voting rights. (Authorities in Alabama had made it very difficult for Black people to register to vote and, in some cases, wouldn't allow them to vote at all.)

Like the Birmingham Children's Crusade, the Selma march met with an overwhelming amount of violence from the authorities. When the marchers attempted to cross the Edmund Pettus Bridge (*pictured*), which led out of Selma across the Alabama River, dozens of state troopers and sheriff's deputies on horseback set upon the peaceful, well-dressed marchers with tear gas, bullwhips, billy clubs, and other weapons. Fifty marchers were hospitalized. Live images of the marchers being beaten were broadcast on prime-time national television, motivating sympathy marches throughout the country and boosting calls for equal voting rights. This led directly to the passage of the national Voting Rights Act of 1965.

King's speech is the iconic event in our collective memory of the 1963 March on Washington.

As US involvement in a faraway conflict grows, the effects spark new types of protest at home.

After the Asian country of Vietnam won its independence from France in 1954, it divided into two parts. North Vietnam declared itself a Communist country. South Vietnam soon fell into a civil war about whether it, too, should become Communist. The United States, which was anti-Communist, sent a small number of combat troops in 1954 to support South Vietnam's anti-Communist government. But as the war grew, the United States became more involved. By 1965 President Lyndon Johnson was calling for 50,000 additional troops to add to the 130,000 already there.

That was just the beginning. At the war's height, more than half a million young US men were fighting in a war that seemed to get more complicated by the day. The war was not popular nationally, and by 1967, most Americans thought it had been a mistake to get involved. Violent images of combat and civilian deaths being transmitted back to the United States by a young generation of photojournalists shocked the nation and motivated many to join the anti-war movement. Pacifist organizations and some religious groups thought the war was immoral.

Although Vietnam was far away, the war directly affected people in the United States because of the selective services draft. The draft forced young men of eligible age and physical health to join the military campaign in Vietnam or risk being arrested. Men were required to carry a draft card to show they had registered for the draft. Considering the high casualty rate of the war, many saw this draft as a death sentence and either fled to Canada or deliberately sought arrest as conscientious objectors. Tens of thousands joined the movement of resistance against the war. Still, 2.2 million men were drafted, and the war would grind on until 1975.

DRAFT-CARD BURNING

In August 1965, after a large anti-war protest in Washington, DC—and hearing reports that men around the country were burning and destroying their draft cards—Congress quickly passed a law that made it illegal to intentionally destroy the cards. The law only encouraged more people to commit the act of civil disobedience.

David Miller, a twenty-two-year-old member of the pacifist Catholic Workers movement helped start a wave of draft-card burnings at anti-war protests. Originally, Miller had mailed his draft card back to the military, refusing to serve. That action put him right at the top of the draft list. When called into the army's offices, he staged a personal protest, walking in a circle outside the building and carrying a sign that read, "End the Draft, Stop the War." After an army officer questioned him, he was let go without being arrested.

But once Congress passed the law that mutilating a draft card was illegal, Miller decided he needed to do something more dramatic to call attention to the peace movement and the toll the draft was taking on young men. Miller seized on the idea to publicly burn his draft card at the International Days of Protest action against the war, a rally and parade put on by labor unions and peace groups around New York City's Battery Park, which would attract thousands of people and several media outlets.

Students in Virginia burn their draft cards to protest the draft.

On October 15, 1965, amid the crowd, he climbed on top of a sound truck, declared the war immoral, and said he wanted to make a political statement. "So here goes," Miller said as he set his draft card on fire. It took a couple of attempts. He first tried with matches, but the wind was too strong, so someone handed him a cigarette lighter.

Time magazine and other media outlets recorded the moment. It became one of the first major symbols of the protest against the war. "There is no threat to peace or security from me or from other protesters," he told *Time*. "The danger lies in blindness to the fact that we have something to say."

Miller was arrested under the new law and sentenced to three years in prison. After his actions, rallies featuring mass draft-card burnings became regular events during the Vietnam War era.

MARCH ON THE PENTAGON

Two years later, the anti-war movement had begun developing a vibrant culture around it, attracting young people with trendy fashions, earnest ideals of peace and love, and a lively sense of humor. With flowing clothing and an antiestablishment energy, the "flower children" hippies were marching on the front lines of the protest movement, experimenting with drugs and staging fantastical events—part joking pranks, part seriously strange—that drew media attention.

The October 1967 March on the Pentagon was an early example of the hippie movement coming together with more established protest organizations. The National Mobilization Committee to End the War in Vietnam (known as Mobe) was a coalition of activist organizations that wanted to grow the anti-war movement by staging more massive protests. The idea behind the March on the Pentagon, the headquarters of the US Department of Defense, was to put on

Vietnam protester George Harris puts carnations into gun barrels outside the Pentagon, symbolizing the peace movement's catchphrase of flower power.

the biggest anti-war march yet, which would display a colorful, somewhat wacky resistance—and yield some of the movement's most indelible images.

On the morning of the march, about one hundred thousand people flooded the city, many of them hippies and other young people, as well as bystanders eager to witness the flair of the new "counterculture." A sense of nervous excitement was in the air, even danger. Abbie Hoffman, cofounder of a theatrical protest group called the Yippies, proclaimed, "We will dye the Potomac [river] red, burn the cherry trees, panhandle embassies, attack with water pistols, marbles, bubble gum wrappers, bazookas . . . Voodoo, warlocks, medicine men, and speed freaks will hurl their magic at the faded brown walls." Some in the crowd hoped to storm the Pentagon and dismantle the military-industrial complex.

They also half-jokingly intended to levitate the building, by forming a circle around the Pentagon and, using their mental energy, actually lifting it off the ground in an "exorcism to cast out evil spirits." None of that happened when about thirty thousand to fifty thousand people branched off to march to the Pentagon. But thousands of heavily armed military police, federal marshals, and army troops met the marchers to stop them from surrounding the building.

Burning Draft Cards, Levitating the Pentagon

YIPPIES IN THE WINGS

Running a pig for president, throwing pies in the faces of politicians, tossing dollar bills onto the New York Stock Exchange trading floor, holding cannabis "smoke-ins" to protest whatever they could think of . . . These were some of the political pranks of the Yippies (*pictured*), a politically focused group of hippies. Trying to levitate the Pentagon fit right into their wild agenda. In 1967 Abbie and Anita Hoffman, Jerry Rubin, Paul Krassner, and Nancy Kurshan founded the Yippies—later called the Youth International Party to sound more official to the media. The Yippies had no hierarchy or central organization, yet they played a big role in political protests against Vietnam, swinging from harmless street theater to violent confrontation.

Photographs of the confrontation between the flower children and the army, with young people holding out chrysanthemum blossoms toward the troops' threatening bayonets, became worldwide symbols, contrasting the nature-oriented, expressive hippie with the uniformed military. The flower children had reached the national stage. Many protesters camped out near the Pentagon overnight but dispersed in the morning.

FREE SPEECH MOVEMENT

Something that connected the Vietnam War protests to the civil rights movement of the early 1960s was the free speech movement. Students on college campuses had been participants and supporters of the civil rights movement—some had become Freedom Riders and marched in protests—and campuses were where young people networked and exchanged new ideas. When the University of California, Berkeley, banned certain forms of political activity, thousands of students rebelled. Led by the fiery Mario Savio and several others, the students faced mass arrests and famously climbed on top of a police car to declare their right to speak freely about politics and world issues. The free speech movement protests lasted a year before university officials backed down and the activists declared victory. Many involved in the movement went on to organize anti-war protests.

Vietnam protesters created posters, buttons, and other artwork to make their voices heard.

CHAPTER 14

SEASON OF THE FLOWER CHILDREN

THE SUMMER OF LOVE, 1967

Hippies dance in San Francisco's Golden Gate Park in April 1967.

Hippies descend on San Francisco's Haight-Ashbury neighborhood to create their own utopia.

Sometimes a protest is a big party. Parties can be powerful opportunities for people to connect with one another, blow off steam through dancing and music, and create an alternative, more welcoming world. They're fun too, and they draw out people who usually wouldn't march in the streets.

The Summer of Love was one *long* party, but it had some earnest intentions behind it. In the spring and summer of 1967, around one hundred thousand people flooded into San Francisco's Haight-Ashbury neighborhood, next to Golden Gate Park. That moment defined the hippie movement—a months-long, media-friendly campout of self-defined "freaks," eager to express their rebellion by coming together and celebrating youth culture.

What were they rebelling against? The hippie movement brought together many kinds of protests happening in the 1950s and 1960s: anti-Vietnam War, civil rights, feminism, gay rights, and economic justice. Some hippies wanted to overthrow capitalism, an economic system they saw as favoring the rich and dooming the poor. Some hippies just wanted to groove to rock music and look cool. (The word *hippie* derives from the slang term *hip*, or cool.)

No matter their motivation, they all came to San Francisco hoping to find something different from their hometowns. Many considered what they were doing to be the opposite of activism. They adopted the mantra "Tune in, turn on, drop out," as a way of rejecting society, choosing to explore their own inner universes through drugs and mystical philosophy. They wanted to escape the pressures of "normal" life and just "be."

In January 1967, a large gathering, the Human Be-In, in Golden Gate Park was designed exactly for those people. Once word about the Human Be-In spread—and after singer Scott McKenzie released a hit record advising people going to San Francisco to wear flowers in their hair—other hippie flower children packed up and headed west.

THE SUMMER OF LOVE

The hippie movement had been gathering steam in the United States and Europe for several years. Vietnam War protests became cultural events that drew thousands of young people, whose lives were affected by the draft. In 1965 one teach-in, part of a broader effort to protest the Vietnam War, had drawn ten thousand people to Berkeley, California, for a thirty-four-hour marathon of speakers, folk music, and political satire. Later that year, an "acid rock" concert drew thousands, who danced all night and protested the war and police brutality. In 1966 in

71

San Francisco, at the Trips Festival, a huge crowd gathered to take the drug LSD, listen to music by the Grateful Dead, and watch a psychedelic light show.

In 1967 the hippies really took off. When police asked a group of hundreds of hippies gathered in New York's Tompkins Square Park to turn down their music, the crowd responded by throwing rocks and bottles. Media coverage of these events, meant to warn parents of the threat of hippie youth, had the opposite effect. "Hippie hysteria" articles attracted even more curious young people. During spring break, people began to stream into Golden Gate Park and stay there.

This surge completely overwhelmed the Haight-Ashbury neighborhood, once a quiet shopping district. San Francisco's population increased by up to 15 percent. Even hippies who had been part of the scene for years felt pushed aside by the influx of young people, TV cameras, tour buses, and street merchants hawking tie-dyed T-shirts, feather hair clips, and cannabis pipes.

An ad for the first Human Be-In in San Francisco, January 1967.

HIPPIE STYLE

The Summer of Love was one of the first large-scale protests driven by youth culture (or, as participants rebelliously called it, "counterculture"), which included unique fashion, music, art, and even food. Outfits combined fluorescent colors, flowing denim, crocheted patterns, large hats, military jackets, and "far-out" designs influenced by psychedelic drug trips. Psychedelic rock by '60s music heroes Jimi Hendrix, Janis Joplin, Jefferson Airplane, the Grateful Dead, and more filled the air. People shared food and belongings, and participants strived to keep everything free. Hippie style was enormously popular. It still enjoys revivals in popular culture, even if the hippie look is often separated from hippie ideals.

FEEDING THE MASSES

How do you feed one hundred thousand people who just show up for a few days (or a few months)? "Free food. Good hot stew. Ripe tomatoes. Fresh fruit. Bring a bowl and spoon," read flyers posted by a community activist group calling themselves the Diggers. Branching off from political street performance group the San Francisco Mime Troupe, the Diggers wanted to clothe, feed, and house people in real life. For months they fed hundreds of people in Golden Gate Park—and operated a free health clinic and a "free store"—until they celebrated the end of the Summer of Love with a comic funeral parade down Haight Street commemorating the "Death of Hippie."

But the scene at the park, at least in the early weeks, fulfilled the hippie promise of utopia. Impromptu dance parties, shared food, theatrical performance troupes, live music, poetry readings, and mystical chanting wove through the crowd like clouds of smoke. Rock and art icons mingled with young kids who had hitchhiked across the country. Long hair decorated with flower crowns and suede vests with bell-bottom jeans were a typical unisex look.

Because the Summer of Love was an organic event rather than a planned one, it didn't accomplish any goals as a protest, but it provided a space for people to live out a personal version of utopia to see what could be possible. However, the lack of planning and structure soon showed the Summer of Love's limits. When money ran out and San Francisco residents began to lose patience, many participants found themselves homeless and begging on the streets. Drug addiction and incidents of sexual abuse and mental illness rose throughout the summer. By October things had taken a darker turn, and the "Death of Hippie" was declared. That didn't stop popular culture, which celebrated the hippie image for decades afterward.

Season of the Flower Children

CHAPTER 15

"NO MORE MISS AMERICA"

THE MISS AMERICA PROTEST, 1968

Feminists protest the famous beauty pageant, and the women's liberation movement gains national exposure.

Women had joined the workforce in droves during World War II, when many men went overseas to fight. This helped to break the stereotype of women as "the weaker sex," whose role was confined to homemaking and raising children. Advances in home technology, such as the washing machine and vacuum, freed up time for more middle-class women to pursue careers or interests outside the home. By the late 1960s, more women were starting businesses, choosing not to be married, and living "unconventional" lives. In turn, society's attitudes about how women should look, dress, behave, and speak were gradually changing.

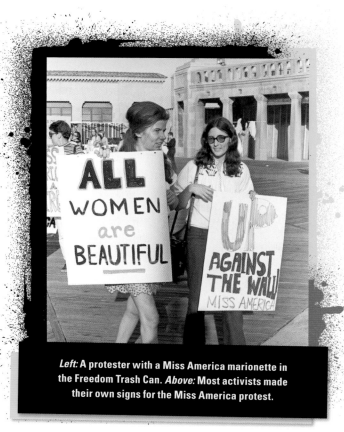

Left: A protester with a Miss America marionette in the Freedom Trash Can. *Above:* Most activists made their own signs for the Miss America protest.

For many women, however, attitudes were not changing fast enough. Since 1923 women's rights organizations had been trying to pass an Equal Rights Amendment to the Constitution, which would legally grant women equal standing with men on matters such as property ownership, employment opportunities and wages, and divorce. Although the Nineteenth Amendment in 1919 gave women the right to vote, Black women continued to face many hurdles to voting because of segregation. It wasn't until the Voting Rights Act of 1965 that they were undeniably able to vote.

In 1968 many women still faced discrimination over what they wore and how they acted. Feminism, the social movement to establish equality for women, was growing stronger as many women realized that stereotypes and men in power were holding them back.

WOMEN'S LIT

Books, essays, newsletters, and other forms of literature powered the women's lib movement. Many of the Miss America protest organizers became notorious for publications that had scandalized the country and shown many women that others thought the way they did. New York Radical Women founder (and former child star) Robin Morgan edited a famous radical feminist book of essays called *Sisterhood Is Powerful*. Shulamith Firestone's groundbreaking book *The Dialectic of Sex: The Case for Feminist Revolution* and her newsletter *Voice of the Women's Liberation Movement* were essential reading. The title of Carol Hanisch's influential essay, "The Personal Is Political," became a slogan of the women's rights movement.

While people were protesting over racial and economic matters, women began to protest for equality and freedom, or women's liberation.

One very visible target for protest was the Miss America pageant, an annual beauty contest that many feminists saw as reinforcing a stereotype that women's beauty was worth more than their brains. (Others believed the contest celebrated "feminine" qualities and was a way for women to earn money as spokesmodels for pageant sponsors.) The New York Radical Women, a feminist group, planned a theatrical protest outside the 1968 pageant in Atlantic City, New Jersey, to bring attention to women's liberation.

THE PROTEST

To prepare for the protest, the group printed a pamphlet, "No More Miss America!" The pamphlet invited every type of woman to join in the one-day action. It warned men to stay away but encouraged sympathetic ones to donate money for the cause or cars to transport women to the protest.

Calling the pageant "The Degrading Mindless-Boob-Girlie Symbol" and characterizing it as a kind of farm animal auction, "No More Miss America!" stated the protesters' case: "The parade down the runway blares the metaphor of the 4-H Club county fair, where the nervous animals are judged for teeth, fleece, etc., and where the best 'Specimen' gets the blue ribbon. So are women in our society forced daily to compete for male approval, enslaved by ludicrous 'beauty' standards we ourselves are conditioned to take seriously."

On September 7, 1968, buses and cars filled with more than three hundred feminists drove toward the pageant site on the Atlantic City boardwalk. The mood was joyful as they sang songs with lyrics including, "Won't be no Miss America no more" and "Sisters, come and join the fight!" As the pageant went on inside Boardwalk Hall, protesters outside rallied with signs that read, "Let's judge ourselves as people" and "Can makeup cover the wounds of our oppression?" A large marionette of a woman in an American flag bathing suit was paraded around and auctioned off. Some protesters entered the pageant itself and unfurled a bedsheet that read "Women's Liberation." While many onlookers of the protest cheered, others jeered. A large contingent of men gathered, hurling homophobic slurs and yelling that the women were crazy Communists.

"Let's judge ourselves as people."

The most iconic part of the protest was the Freedom Trash Can, a large garbage bin into which women threw items that symbolized oppression to them: bras, girdles, curlers, false eyelashes, wigs, and women's magazines. One reporter on the scene falsely wrote that women were burning their bras. This image came to symbolize the feminist movement and caused scandal across the country, itself becoming a stereotype of "angry feminists."

The protest grabbed national attention and electrified the feminist movement. In the years that followed, the Equal Rights Amendment gained a wave of support and the House and Senate approved it. However, the required number of states failed to ratify it, so it was not added to the Constitution.

GET ON THE BUS

Transportation can sometimes be a real problem during a protest. How do you get everybody where they need to be? Sometimes you have to be resourceful. When Miss America protest organizer Robin Morgan arrived at the meeting point to board a bus for Atlantic City, she was shocked to find three hundred women had turned up. "I remember rushing to a phone booth—this was before smart phones, of course—and desperately trying to order more buses," Morgan told an interviewer. "But the only ones I could find at the last minute were the kind that transported Hasidic Jewish men from their Brooklyn neighborhoods to the jewelry district in Manhattan. So a number of us traveled to Atlantic City in buses decorated in all Hebrew symbols. I think the Orthodox Jewish drivers were traumatized by the songs the women were singing!"

FISTS RAISED FOR BLACK POWER

FREE HUEY RALLIES, 1968–1970

Black Panther party members demonstrate outside a New York City courthouse in April 1969.

The Black Panthers stage militant protests to free their leader.

The civil rights movement brought about great changes in segregation laws. But the experience of the Freedom Riders showed that changing the law didn't automatically mean changing society. Deeply rooted racism and prejudice continued to frustrate Black communities. Equality and economic opportunity still felt out of reach.

Some Black activists questioned Martin Luther King Jr.'s emphasis on nonviolent protest and working within the US government system. Influential figure Malcolm X rejected the goal of racial integration, advocating for the ideas of Black separatism and achieving liberation by any means necessary. The Black Power movement drew on some of his ideas, emphasizing Black pride, self-sufficiency, and independence.

The Black Panther Party for Self-Defense was born from this separatist idea and attempted to empower Black communities to rely more on themselves. Founded in 1966 in Oakland, California, by Huey Newton and Bobby Seale, the group was originally concerned with how to monitor and prevent police brutality. Oakland in the 1960s was a conservative, working-class city with a large Black population that felt terrorized by the local police force. The Black Panthers came together to keep a close eye on the police, "copwatching" with their own guns and law books at the ready and intervening in suspicious situations.

From there, the Black Panthers grew to encompass other social justice issues. Their philosophy of revolutionary socialism and Black Power drew attention from around the country, and the group issued the Ten-Point Program, a manifesto that demanded access to housing, food, clothing, education, and fair trials. The group then set out to enact some of its goals by launching more than sixty community programs that provided, among other things, free breakfast for children, free health clinics, free clothes and shoes, and a free school. Soon there were Black Panther Party chapters in major US cities.

Fearful of armed Black Panthers monitoring the Oakland police, the California legislature moved to pass a gun control law that would forbid people from carrying loaded weapons in public. To protest this bill, the Vietnam War, and police brutality, more than two dozen armed Black Panthers, holding rifles and shotguns, entered the California State Capitol in 1967. While legal at the time, their action shocked a country that had grown used to nonviolent sit-ins and marches and produced a political backlash. California governor Ronald Reagan passed the gun control bill, and FBI director J. Edgar Hoover began to target the Black Panthers as enemies of the country, ordering the party's leaders followed and harassed.

Fists Raised for Black Power

A group of boys and young men give the Black Power salute.

Yet with their sleek leather jackets, cocked berets, dark sunglasses, and Black Power salutes (holding one fist in the air), the Panthers became a pop culture phenomenon that the media couldn't resist. Oppression of the Black Panthers only seemed to increase their image as revolutionary renegades fighting against an overwhelming system. They polished this image at a series of rallies held to free one of their leaders from prison.

THE RALLIES

On October 28, 1967, Oakland police pulled over Black Panthers founder Huey Newton. A shootout occurred that left officer John Frey dead and Newton critically injured. Even though Newton had no weapon on him, he was arrested and charged with murder, assault, and kidnapping. While he was imprisoned awaiting trial, Newton became an international symbol of resistance against racism. For the next three years—until the charges were dropped and he was released—"Free Huey" became a rallying cry.

In February 1968, the Black Panthers held the first in a series of Free Huey rallies. It was Newton's birthday, and more than five thousand people filled the Oakland Auditorium, listening to speeches from Black Power figures including Seale, Stokely Carmichael, and Eldridge Cleaver and enjoying entertainment and food. More rallies followed, including another large one in nearby San Francisco in May 1969. During the rallies, Black Panthers marched in unison in a military style and chanted slogans, such as "Black is beautiful," "Revolution has come, time to pick up the gun," and "All power to the people."

At the time Newton's trial began in July 1968, the rallies were drawing sympathetic Latino, Asian, and white protesters, many of them Berkeley college students. Outside the Alameda courthouse where the case was being heard, protesters held up copies of a well-known picture of Newton seated on a wicker throne, holding a rifle and sporting the typical Black Panthers beret and leather jacket uniform.

The Free Huey rallies helped amplify the Black Power message of the Panthers, connected with other armed struggles against government oppression around the globe, and spawned an art, music, literature, film, and fashion movement that looked to Black culture and African history for inspiration. The rallies provided unity during a very turbulent period in Black American history. Malcolm X had been assassinated in 1965, Martin Luther King Jr. was assassinated in 1968, and Black community uprisings and racial violence from Detroit to Los Angeles had marked the end of the civil rights movement period.

After Newton's release in 1970, the Panthers continued their mission for several more years but violent infighting and a lack of steady income plagued the Panthers. Newton died in a fight in 1981, but many of the other Panthers became well-known educators, lawyers, authors, and even fashion designers. Black Panther organizers Kathleen Cleaver and Angela Davis became important feminist leaders.

BRANDING THE BLACK PANTHERS

Imagery and artwork were just as important as spreading the Black Panthers' message of people power to the world. The group's minister of culture Emory Douglas was the graphic design mastermind behind most of the organization's pamphlets, posters, and the *Black Panther* newspaper. His simple but powerful designs were considered "militant-chic," in that they carried a deep revolutionary message yet were visually appealing.

Striking posters of rebel fighters, such as Cuba's Che Guevara, or powerful women holding guns, often accented with neon pinks, greens, and yellows, vibrated with revolutionary fervor. Illustrations of schoolchildren eating free breakfast or receiving new clothes emphasized the Panthers' community mission. Most of the party's literature was marked with the Black Panthers logo (a crouching black panther, of course), which was an early form of political branding.

CHAPTER 17

CHAOS IN CHICAGO

DEMOCRATIC NATIONAL CONVENTION PROTESTS, 1968

Of the tens of thousands of protesters at the Democratic National Convention in 1968,

Clashes erupt and pigs run for president as Vietnam protests continue at the height of the war.

Fear, frustration, and rebellion were in the air in the summer of 1968. The Vietnam War was raging, and so were protests against it. Uprisings, many of them violent, were overwhelming major cities, as Black people fought back against economic oppression and were crushed by the military. An assassin took the life of Martin Luther King Jr. in April, and another killed Senator Robert Kennedy in June. It felt as if anything could happen.

In the lead-up to the Democratic Party's national convention in Chicago, things looked bleak. Democratic president Lyndon Johnson decided not to run again. Anti-war activists had pushed for a new Democratic president who would listen to the growing protests around the country and bring US troops home from Vietnam. But their hopes were dashed when the party looked set to nominate Johnson's vice president, Hubert Humphrey, without even going through the proper voting process. This undemocratic decision made many people feel as though participation in the election—and the current system of US government—was useless.

THE PROTESTS

Protesters descended on Chicago in late July, full of rambunctious spirit and a nothing-to-lose attitude. Protests were organized by a coalition of activists from Mobe and the Yippies, who were joined by Black Panthers leader Bobby Seale. Ten thousand mostly young people swarmed Lincoln Park. They paraded their squealing nominee for president, a pig named Pigasus the Immortal, through the crowd. Yoga sessions, rock bands, and dance parties showcased the new flower child spirit that was sweeping youth culture. Protesters figured that if the political establishment wouldn't hear them, then at least a media spectacle would ensure the rest of the country did.

Protesters battle police at the 1968 Democratic National Convention.

The Chicago police, however, had different ideas. They attacked the crowd, throwing tear gas and beating the protesters. Later, on August 28, fifteen thousand protesters showed up at Grant Park for a demonstration at the band shell. When a teenage boy climbed a flagpole and lowered the American flag, police seized him. Protesters threw food and rocks at the officers. The police beat and teargassed them as well.

Many protesters headed away from the violent scene to the Hilton Hotel, where Humphrey and other convention participants were staying. There, a standoff between thousands of protesters and thousands of police took place. Suddenly, chaos—the police once again savagely beat and gassed the protesters, alarming the public watching on the news.

By the end of the convention, more than 650 people were arrested and more than 200 were treated for injuries. Police arrested leaders of the Yippies and the Mobe, as well as Seale, and charged them with trying to incite a riot. The famous trial of these Chicago Eight was a

THE MORATORIUM TO END THE WAR IN VIETNAM

On October 15, 1969, more than two million people joined in demonstrations around the world to protest the Vietnam War. Many marched in major cities, including New York, Detroit, Boston, and Miami, wearing black armbands, a symbol of mourning. This *moratorium*—a strong declaration that forbids something, in this case war—was a massive effort that also included a teach-in, which combined debates, discussions, movies, musical performances, and scholarly lectures about the war and how to protest it.

A November demonstration in Washington, DC, followed. Here, the Mobe held a solemn March against Death, walking single file from Arlington Cemetery to the Capitol, each person carrying a sign with the name of a US soldier killed in the war or a destroyed Vietnamese village. The signs were placed in coffins and taken to the White House by parents of dead soldiers, anti-war veterans, religious leaders, and Congress members who opposed the war.

At a huge cultural festival afterward, half a million people turned up outside the White House. Outspoken anti-war folk music acts Arlo Guthrie and Peter, Paul and Mary played. Singer Pete Seeger led the crowd in a sing-along of John Lennon's new song "Give Peace a Chance."

chaotic circus, with Yippies disrupting the proceedings as much as possible to protest the false charges. They were cleared, but their tactics and the pandemonium of the convention did little to stop the war. Richard Nixon, the Republican candidate, was elected president.

TRAGEDY AT KENT STATE

College campuses had been centers of protests against the Vietnam War since the US had become involved, and clashes between students and authorities were common. One demonstration turned deadly when the Ohio National Guard fired into a crowd of protesters, killing four young people.

In 1970 the war seemed to be finally winding down. President Richard Nixon had been elected on a promise to end it and was already withdrawing more than a hundred thousand troops. In April, however, Nixon ordered a secret, illegal bombing campaign on neighboring country Cambodia, where he thought North Vietnamese forces were hiding.

Enraged by this unlawful act, which killed up to half a million people, the students of Ohio's Kent State University staged several days of protests. One of the protests became destructive, and students burned down the campus ROTC (Reserve Officers' Training Corps) building. The Ohio governor, who detested the protests, stationed the National Guard around the campus.

During a May 4 protest, some students threw rocks at the National Guardsmen. Without warning, the battalion turned around and fired at students. Four students—Jeffrey Miller, Allison Krause, William Schroeder, and Sandra Scheuer—were killed. Nine more were seriously injured. The Guard shot some of the students in the back.

The National Guard later admitted it was wrong to fire at the students. But photos published in newspapers the next day of unarmed students murdered on campus by state security forces stunned the country. Although it would be another three years until the war officially ended, national opinion had decisively soured on it.

The moratorium marchers in Boston, October 1969

CHAPTER 18

RIOTING FOR GAY LIBERATION

THE STONEWALL RIOTS, 1969

A community forced to live in shadows proudly stands up to the police.

In the 1960s, lesbian, gay, bisexual, transgender people, and those questioning their sexual orientation or assigned gender (now known as the LGBTQ community but back then usually just called gay) faced severe legal and social discrimination.

Gay bars, gay parties, and gay sex were illegal in most states. Dressing in clothes not considered "correct" for a person's assumed gender could lead to prison or shame on the front page of the local newspaper. If their identities were publicized, LGBTQ people could lose their careers and homes. Since homosexuality was officially classified as a mental disorder, the authorities (and sometimes their own families) sent many gay people to mental institutions. Believing gay people to be susceptible to blackmail and Communist influence, the US government had declared homosexuals a security risk in the 1950s and purged thousands of people from government jobs.

But a vibrant LGBTQ subculture existed. As with other minority communities, the subculture wanted recognition and social justice. Underground organizations such as the Mattachine Society in Los Angeles and the Daughters of Bilitis in San Francisco advocated for acceptance of homosexuals and eventually grew into national organizations. In April 1965, these two groups staged the first public gay and lesbian political demonstrations outside the White House and the United Nations, to call attention to the imprisonment of gay people in Cuba.

Hundreds of gay bars, nightclubs, theaters, and gathering places existed as well, in spite of being illegal. The Mafia operated many bars and clubs, especially in New York City. While the Mafia paid bribes and kickbacks to corrupt police officers to keep their illegal gathering places in business, police raids still happened.

Gay patrons, caught in these raids, were blackmailed and violently harassed. In August 1966 in San Francisco, a group of transgender women fought back against the police intimidation in what became the Compton's Cafeteria riot. In 1967 in Los Angeles, patrons of the gay Black Cat tavern held a demonstration after police beat and arrested fourteen people there on New Year's Eve. These events set the stage for the largest LGBTQ protest of the early gay civil rights era, the Stonewall Riots.

The Stonewall Inn in New York City's Greenwich Village was a bar often targeted by police. It catered to a diverse, younger clientele, many of whom embraced the countercultural spirit of the 1960s and its emphasis on social justice and individual expression.

THE RIOTS

"Police! We're taking the place!" came the cry from the Stonewall Inn door at 1:20 a.m. on Saturday, June 28, 1969. The police burst into the crowded bar, and the lights came on, revealing more than two hundred people inside. Police barred their escape from the windows and doors, demanded identification from patrons, and separated transgender people into a group for officers to take into the bathroom to "confirm" their birth gender.

Unlike at previous raids, the Stonewall patrons refused to strip naked or to produce identification. In their confusion, police decided to arrest many of them and take them downtown to police headquarters. But a crowd had gathered outside to watch what was happening and heckle the officers. Witnesses say the atmosphere was a mixture of humor and hostility. But when a police officer hit a lesbian over the head as she was led out of Stonewall, she reportedly yelled to the crowd, "Why don't you guys do something?" The crowd, which had grown to more than five hundred people, began rioting, joined by more people from other gay bars in the area and bystanders on the street. Rioters chanted "gay power" and attempted to overturn police vehicles and slash tires.

Police officers try to push back protesters outside the Stonewall Inn on June 28, 1969.

The riots became a spectacle, lasting five more days. They attracted huge crowds that protested for gay rights and visibility, while showing what was then scandalous public affection and continuing to battle with police. The protests attracted all strata of gay New York society, from street prostitutes to famous writers—even tourists showed up. Like many such social actions, not everyone in the community approved. The outspokenness and diversity of Stonewall clashed with the clean-cut, more "acceptable" vision of homosexuals that older gay rights organizations hoped to project to win the public's approval.

With their diversity and radical approach, the Stonewall riots are widely considered the flash point of the contemporary LGBTQ rights movement, which has brought everything from the decriminalization of sodomy laws to same-sex marriage. Immediately following the riots, several radical gay publications and organizations formed, including the Gay Liberation Front, the first organization with the word *gay* in its name. The next year, LGBTQ people gathered in cities across the country to commemorate the riots in Gay Freedom Day picnics and parties, which later became the huge, worldwide Gay Pride or LGBTQ Pride marches and celebrations.

> **The crowd, which had grown to more than five hundred people, began rioting, joined by more people from other gay bars in the area and bystanders on the street.**

KICKING UP THEIR HEELS

Musical theater was a big part of gay culture at the time of Stonewall. Famous musical star Judy Garland had died just days earlier, and much of the crowd was in mourning. So the protest songs and chants during the riots were especially theatrical. LGBTQ people at the riots formed lines, linked arms, kicked up their legs in unison, and chanted, *"We are the Stonewall Girls / We wear our hair in curls. / We wear no underwear / We show our pubic hairs."* It was a bawdy act of cultural defiance in the face of armed authority.

ON THE FRONT LINES

SYLVIA RIVERA (1951–2002)

Called the Rosa Parks of the transgender movement, Sylvia Rivera was a civil rights, anti-Vietnam War, and feminist activist who participated in the riots. Along with her friend Marsha P. Johnson, Rivera later became one of the most prominent voices for gay and transgender liberation, starting several organizations and advocating for diversity and tolerance.

MARSHA P. JOHNSON (1945–1992)

Outspoken transgender activist and model Marsha P. Johnson was known as the mayor of Christopher Street, the street where the Stonewall Inn stood. One of the most prominent participants in the riots, she cofounded the Gay Liberation Front gay rights organization immediately afterward. With Sylvia Rivera, Johnson formed the transgender advocacy group Street Transvestite Action Revolutionaries in 1970.

The second annual Gay Pride March in New York, on June 27, 1971, celebrated the anniversary of the Stonewall Riots.

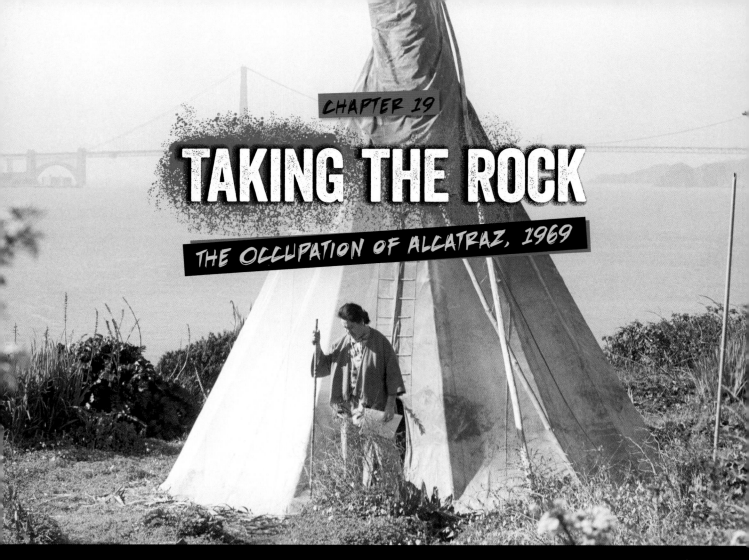

CHAPTER 19

TAKING THE ROCK

THE OCCUPATION OF ALCATRAZ, 1969

An activist stands in front of a tepee on Alcatraz Island during the occupation.

Native Americans reclaim a California island to protest treatment by the US government.

Mayday! Mayday! The Indians have landed!" That was what the security guard yelled as eighty-nine Native Americans in small boats invaded the island of Alcatraz, the former site of a notorious prison known as the Rock, one night in November 1969. But the story of why these activists would want to take over a desolate little spot in the middle of the San Francisco Bay starts long before that.

Throughout the history of the United States, its government had pressured American Indians to live on smaller and smaller areas of land, either through negotiation or by force. By the middle of the twentieth century, many of those living on Indian reservations—separated from one another by distance and tribal tradition, and often denied participation in the US economy—experienced high levels of poverty and lack of jobs or opportunity.

During the 1950s, the US government adopted policies that focused on Indian relocation. These policies were intended to move Native Americans from reservations into cities, where they could receive job training, housing, and access to medical insurance. Trusting the government and searching for a better life, tens of thousands of Native Americans left their rural communities for big cities. In Northern California, many came to Oakland and San Francisco.

But the relocation policies backfired in several ways. The Native Americans who moved into new communities often faced prejudice and segregation, and they lived in the same poor conditions that they had fled. Worse, the US government broke many promises, such as job training and money for housing. Some Native Americans felt tricked into leaving their land and culture behind in an attempt to destroy their identity and heritage.

Native American activists had been watching the civil rights movement closely. The American Indian Movement (AIM) formed in 1968 to help those American Indians who had moved into poor neighborhoods, and it grew to advocate for economic independence, legal rights, a reawakening of cultural traditions, and connections among people from different nations and tribes. AIM also demanded restoration of American Indian lands that it believed were illegally seized by the US government, as well as the right to govern those lands free of government interference. The organization set out to use similar strategies as the civil rights movement to achieve those goals.

Inspired by AIM and reeling from a fire that destroyed their cultural center in San Francisco, a group of American Indians came together, setting their sights on taking over Alcatraz as a symbolic protest that would get the country's attention. These activists were highly influenced by San Francisco's theatrical protest scene, so they knew how well something both dramatic and colorful could help their cause.

Why Alcatraz? The chilly, creepy island prison had closed in 1963. Citing an 1868 treaty that entitled American Indians to reclaim federal lands that were no longer in use, five Sioux activists had attempted to take the island over in 1964, to make a point that the United States should honor its treaties. Ever since that mission failed, taking the Rock had been a goal for Native American activists. As activist Richard Oakes put it, explaining that Alcatraz is the first thing that people see when they sail into San Francisco, "This tiny island would be a symbol of the great lands once ruled by free and noble Indians."

THE OCCUPATION

Oakes, a member of the Mohawk tribe, and a group of others dressed in tribal regalia attempted to reclaim Alcatraz on November 9, 1969. They jumped from a boat and swam to the island,

BROADCASTING THE OCCUPATION

Using borrowed and donated equipment, John Trudell—a Santee Sioux from Nebraska—set up a makeshift radio station, Radio Free Alcatraz. Several other radio stations in the area boosted its signal, increasing its power. His daily broadcasts consisted of news, music, and interviews from the island. Each episode began with a recording of Buffy Sainte-Marie singing the Native protest song, "Now That the Buffalo's Gone."

John Trudell (*right*) interviews Grace Thorpe for a Radio Free Alcatraz broadcast.

making headlines and inspiring others, even though the Coast Guard removed them from Alcatraz the next day. Oakes's action drew the attention of student activists and a broad representation of American Indian society. On November 20, a large group assembled in the coastal town of Sausalito to try again.

Boarding a small assortment of boats borrowed from sympathetic bar owners and sailors, the eighty-nine activists—men, women, and children—set sail as dark fell. When they reached the island, ignoring armed Coast Guard boats and the panicked cries of the guards, they immediately moved to occupy the former prison warden's residence and other buildings. To claim the space, they spray-painted graffiti messages on the prison walls, including "Peace and Freedom," "Welcome," and "Home of the Free Indian Land."

Soon hundreds more Native activists from many tribes were sailing to Alcatraz to join the occupation, leaving their homes across Northern California. The island became a fully functional village whose population swelled to around five hundred. LaNada Means, of the Shoshone Bannock people, was the village's main organizer; Stella Leach, of the Lakota/Colville people, ran the health clinic; and Grace Thorpe, of Sac and Fox tribal descent, worked to bring the Alcatraz message to the wider world by recruiting celebrities to come see the island community for themselves.

The island had its own radio station and hosted musical performances. Supporters delivered supplies by canoe. Despite some hardships—Alcatraz had no fresh water source, and soon so many people were arriving that it began to get overcrowded—the occupation was at first a success story. Thousands of people came to visit and assist the occupation.

The occupiers named themselves the Indians of All Tribes. They issued a formal proclamation declaring that Alcatraz would host a new cultural center and school—and mockingly offered the US government twenty-four dollars in beads and cloth for the land, which is what colonists had paid for the island of Manhattan in 1626.

President Richard Nixon ignored the occupation at first, but as it became a celebrity cause and stretched out for more than a year, he realized he had to address it. Some on Nixon's staff, including Vice President Spiro Agnew, were sympathetic to the occupation and convinced the president to restrain from using force. Nixon offered instead to build the American Indians a park elsewhere, which they initially refused, demanding money to rebuild the island.

After nineteen months, the occupation ran out of steam. Internal conflicts arose among the island's leaders, most of the student occupiers went back to school, and the lack of water and steady electricity—frequently shut off by the government—made life difficult on Alcatraz. Finally, on June 11, 1971, Nixon sent in troops to evict the remaining occupiers, and the island later became a tourist museum.

However, the utopian community left a lasting impact. For the first time in the twentieth century, such a large group of people from different Native tribes came together to protest their treatment. The Alcatraz occupation influenced future protests, including the Occupation of Wounded Knee (see chapter 21) and the Occupy movement (see chapter 28). Beyond that, the occupation also produced actual change. Over the next four years, the Nixon administration transferred millions of acres of land and dedicated more than a billion dollars in funds to American Indian projects, culminating in the 1975 Indian Self-Determination and Education Assistance Act, which gave American Indian nations more control over their lands and government funding.

STAR POWER

Grace Thorpe, a World War II veteran from Oklahoma and the daughter of famed athlete Jim Thorpe, helped spread the word about the occupation by making it a celebrity event covered by global media. She organized visits to Alcatraz from some of the biggest celebrities of the time, including actors Jane Fonda, Marlon Brando, and Anthony Quinn; comedian Dick Gregory; and singer Buffy Sainte-Marie. She also enlisted financial help from famous rock stars such as Creedence Clearwater Revival. The band donated a boat to the cause.

CHAPTER 20

A REVOLT BEHIND BARS

THE ATTICA PRISON UPRISING, 1971

Attica inmates raise their fists in support of their uprising while their leaders negotiate with prison officials.

Inmates seize command of their prison in a doomed effort to demand humane treatment.

What rights are prisoners entitled to—even ones sentenced to the harshest prisons? A violent confrontation brought this question to the fore in 1971 at the Attica Correctional Facility, a fortresslike maximum security prison in New York that was infamous for its severe treatment of inmates.

Attica, built in 1931 specifically to prevent prison riots, was the most expensive, state-of-the-art prison in the country, with walls 2 feet (0.6 m) thick and 30 feet (9 m) tall. The prison had incarcerated some notorious bank robbers and Mafia hit men, but by the 1960s, the facilities were overcrowded and broken down.

By then, Attica housed mostly poor men of color, although all but one of the prison guards were white. Prisoners spent fourteen hours a day in cramped cells, in a dehumanizing atmosphere with inadequate medical care and recreation, barely edible food, and little training or education that would help them reenter society. Attica allowed each prisoner only one shower a week and one roll of toilet paper a month.

Attica banned political organizations and literature, as well as religious services held by Black Muslims, a significant part of the prison population. These restrictions led to an atmosphere of extreme tension. Riots and prison takeovers had happened at other large correctional facilities in 1970, and prison officials transferred some of the participants to Attica. Administrators knew Attica prisoners were angry and feared that the same would happen there.

Yet inmates staged peaceful protests in the summer of 1971, attempting to persuade Russell Oswald, the commissioner of correctional services, to hear their complaints. Oswald visited the prison in early September but left before making any changes.

THE UPRISING

By late September, the prison was a tinderbox waiting for a spark to ignite it. During a particularly chaotic morning on September 9, 1971, a group of prisoners had accidentally been locked in an underground tunnel leading to the outside yard. Thinking they were about to be beaten, they panicked and rioted to break free. Once other prisoners heard what was happening, they joined the rioting. The prisoners armed themselves and rampaged through the prison, beating guards, raiding the kitchen and drug dispensary, and taking hostages. The thirteen hundred prisoners gained control of Attica, holding forty-two staff members hostage.

A Revolt behind Bars

The Attica prison yard after the uprising was crushed

In the four days that followed, prisoners gathered in the outdoor D yard and built their own society. They gave speeches, elected leaders, shared meals, and voted on rules. During the rioting, one guard had been hit in the head and trampled to death. After that, the prisoners vowed to treat their hostages nonviolently and invited outside observers into the prison to relay messages to the outside world. Challenges still existed, however. Isolated instances of rape and beatings among prisoners occurred. Fellow inmates killed three men.

The prisoners issued an elaborate and thoughtful manifesto of demands as a blueprint for humane treatment of inmates throughout the prison system. These demands included better medical care and food, a minimum wage, an end to religious and political persecution, ways to hold violent prison guards accountable, the right to legal representation, the right to form a labor union, better visitor center facilities, and ways for the prisoners to earn money to support their families.

The uprising caught the nation's attention, first with its violence and then with the calm, determined orderliness of the revolt. Young leader Elliott James "L. D." Barkley declaimed to television cameras, "We are men! We are not beasts and we do not intend to be driven or beaten as such!"

It looked as though the negotiations were succeeding. But Oswald and authorities refused to grant amnesty to the prisoners, which meant the protesters would probably be punished for the uprising.

This was too much for the prisoners, and they called off negotiations. New York governor Nelson Rockefeller, who had been loudly against the prisoners' cause and refused to visit the prison, authorized the use of the National Guard and police to attack the prison and rescue the hostages. The prisoners led the blindfolded hostages into the yard and armed themselves with whatever they could. Fearing the hostages would be executed, Oswald ordered an assault on Attica.

On September 13, tear gas was dropped in the yard and state troopers burst in, blindly firing their guns through clouds of smoke. In the chaos that followed, thirty-three inmates and nine hostages were killed, all but one by the troopers' bullets. Dozens more lay wounded. Prisoners later reported that troopers beat and kicked the wounded and shot Barkley in the back.

THE AFTERMATH

State authorities regained control of the prison and lied about the assault, blaming prisoners for the deaths. The prisoners who had participated in the uprising were beaten and criminally charged. Troopers even smashed their eyeglasses and dentures in retaliation.

But much of the public came to view the violent assault as an overreaction and a mistake. An official state report on the events commented that it was "the bloodiest one-day encounter between Americans since the Civil War, with the exception of the Indian massacres in the late nineteenth century." Another stated that the charges against the prisoners were one-sided and that the troopers had engaged in criminal acts of brutality.

The Attica uprising helped galvanize the prisoners' rights movement and drew attention to the state of incarceration facilities nationwide. Later, the New York State Department of Corrections instituted a grievance process for inmates to file complaints about their living situation. The president of the correction officers' union called for more humane facilities and new ways of thinking about incarceration.

Inmates, however, are still calling attention to treatment within prisons. The United States incarcerates more people than any nation in the world, and private companies rather than the public run many prisons. Prisoners still can't vote to change their situation, so strikes and protests occur regularly.

In 2013 thirty thousand prisoners in California went on a hunger strike to protest the practice of solitary confinement and demand better living conditions. In 2016 a nationwide prisoners' strike marked the forty-fifth anniversary of the Attica uprising, protesting what prisoners described as abusive labor conditions. In 2018 prisoners went on strike in seventeen states to demand higher pay for jobs they performed, such as fighting fires. They were being paid less than two dollars an hour.

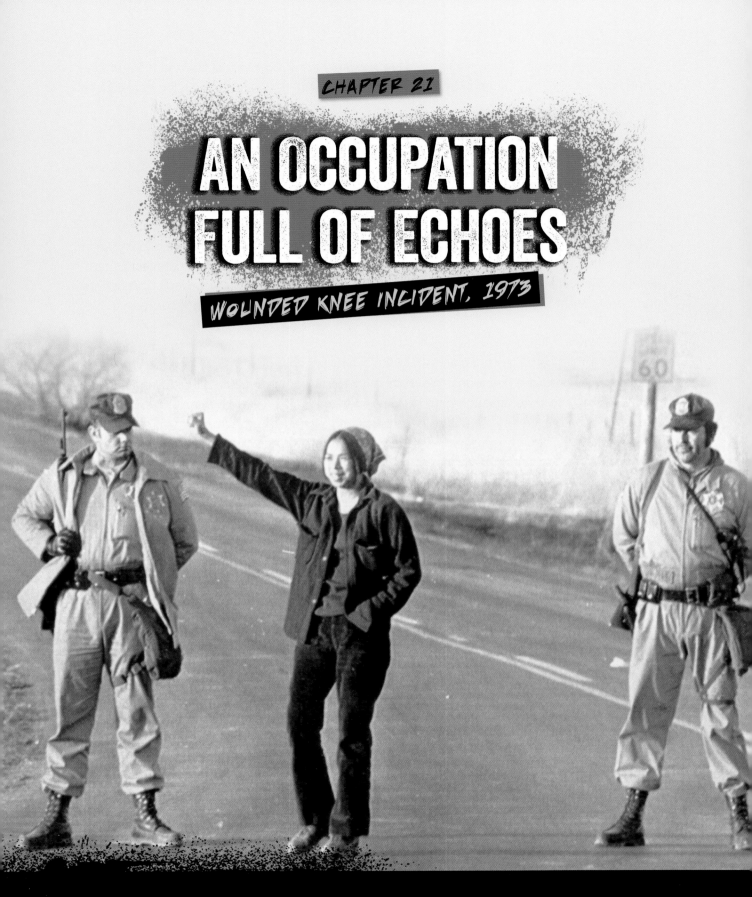

CHAPTER 21

AN OCCUPATION FULL OF ECHOES

WOUNDED KNEE INCIDENT, 1973

Two federal marshals block an access road to Wounded Knee while an activist raises her fist in solidarity with other protesters.

Oglala Lakota activists occupy a town with a dark history, demanding justice from the US government.

In 1890, on the central plains of the continent, US troops killed more than 240 members of the Lakota Sioux in a violent response to a new ritual. Desperate to hold on to their land and culture in the face of US aggression, some Lakota had adopted a form of spiritual practice called the Ghost Dance. Participants in this ritual of protest and empowerment believed it foretold the return of ancient ancestors who would banish white men and restore the traditional way of life. Ghost Dancers also believed they could wear magic shirts that would stop bullets, which made them feel brave.

US authorities felt threatened by the Ghost Dance and its potential to incite rebellion. They ordered the arrest of famous Sioux chief Sitting Bull, who had allowed the Ghost Dance on his Standing Rock Indian Reservation. Sitting Bull died in the ensuing scuffle. Fearing for their lives, several hundred Lakota fled. The US Cavalry stopped them and herded them into a camp along Wounded Knee Creek. The cavalry trained large guns on the camp in case of an uprising.

When some Lakota threw dirt in the air to begin a Ghost Dance, cavalry soldiers panicked and thought they were preparing for an attack. The soldiers moved in on the camp to stop it. A rifle went off, and soldiers began firing, killing dozens, including their own men. The soldiers hunted down and sometimes shot from behind those Lakota who tried to flee along the creek.

Although not the biggest massacre of indigenous peoples in US history, what happened at Wounded Knee became a deeply emotional symbol of the struggle for American Indian survival and self-determination.

A CONTEMPORARY OCCUPATION

Flash forward to 1973. Native peoples were still seeking justice for previous massacres and recognition of treaties signed hundreds of years ago by the US government. The taking of Alcatraz in 1969 had galvanized the American Indian Movement (AIM), uniting tribes and activists into pushing harder for recognition of their demands.

Near Wounded Knee, now a US town in South Dakota, the Oglala band of the Lakota Sioux tribe was also dealing with other problems on their Pine Ridge Reservation. Both the reservation and Wounded Knee had very high rates of poverty and short life expectancies. Many on the reservation accused Dick Wilson, the tribal chairperson, of corruption and armed intimidation, saying he favored mixed-race residents over full-blooded American Indians for government positions and funds. However, they had failed to remove Wilson through democratic means.

An Occupation Full of Echoes

So they turned for help to leaders of AIM, who saw a chance to mobilize the unhappy tribe members and make a larger statement.

On the night of February 27, two hundred armed AIM activists and people from the reservation boarded trucks and entered Wounded Knee, taking the town's residents hostage with very little resistance. AIM leaders Russell Means, an Oglala Lakota, and Dennis Banks, an Ojibwa, declared the town an independent Oglala Sioux

Two protesters stand guard against federal marshals at Wounded Knee.

Nation, vowing to hold the town until the US government met their demands. These included reviewing and honoring all treaties, launching an investigation into the treatment of American Indians, and a change of tribal leadership.

Immediately after the invasion of Wounded Knee, federal marshals surrounded the town. Federal officials later called it the longest-lasting civil disorder in US history up to that point. For the next seventy-one days, occupiers and authorities traded bursts of heavy gunfire. The marshals cut off the town's electricity and water and did what they could to prevent the activists from obtaining food and more ammunition.

But Means and Banks were well known from previous resistance actions. They attracted broad public support with their media skills and glamorous personalities. (Both of them went on to star in movies later in life.) They and other AIM leaders realized that the history of Wounded Knee was a powerful symbol and a ready-made story for news coverage. Like Alcatraz, the Wounded Knee siege drew support from celebrities, activists, and musicians including Jane Fonda, Johnny Cash, Angela Davis, and Marlon Brando, who famously declined an Academy Award in protest of the treatment of American Indians. A sympathetic airplane pilot dropped 2,000 pounds (907 kg) of food into the town to feed the activists.

For their part, the federal authorities surrounding the town amassed so many weapons that it reminded observers of the Vietnam War. "They were shooting machine gun fire at us, tracers coming at us at nighttime just like a war zone," one activist said. "We had some Vietnam vets with us, and they said, 'Man, this is just like Vietnam.'"

Among the arsenal were military-grade grenade launchers, as well as armored cars, helicopters, and snipers. The authorities shot at activists whenever they left the cover of buildings. The first activist to die was "shot by a bullet that flew through the wall of a church."

Remarkably, only two activists were killed throughout the siege (one marshal was shot and paralyzed), but that was enough for the Lakota tribe to end the standoff. Both sides reached an agreement to disarm on May 5, and the activists quietly left the town over the next three days on foot, under cover of darkness. Many, however, were eventually arrested, including Means. They were later released due to mishandling of evidence, a public relations disaster for authorities.

Although the Wounded Knee occupiers brought greater attention to AIM during the "incident," as it became known, rates of poverty and violence on the reservation remained high, and Pine Ridge counts among the poorest areas within US borders. Wounded Knee remains associated with both American Indian tragedy and activism, but the region's turbulent history wasn't over. Nearby Standing Rock Indian Reservation would play a role in the Dakota Access Pipeline protests of 2016, which combined environmental activism and demonstrations for American Indian land rights. (See chapter 31.)

IDENTITY AS POWER

Taking inspiration from the Black civil rights movement—but often moving in a more radical, confrontational direction—many protests in the 1960s and 1970s focused on ethnic or other personal identities. AIM, the Chicano movement, the gay liberation movement, the women's liberation movement, the Black Power movement, and other movements helped channel frustration about the treatment of minorities and other oppressed communities into national actions. These movements and the many organizations that comprised them empowered participants to celebrate their unique heritage and culture while challenging and changing US history.

Other important movements focused on poverty, youth rights, care of veterans, and religious freedom, which intersected with those based on ethnic, sexual, and gender identity. A complex landscape of protests and demands formed, which could be confusing to people who had never previously questioned the way things worked. Often a political or even violent backlash resulted, and some movements embraced these violent tactics. But the civil rights movement propelled an era of self-expression and cultural identification that continues through recent protests such as the 2017 Women's March (see chapter 32) and the young peoples' 2018 March for Our Lives (see chapter 34).

An Occupation Full of Echoes

CHAPTER 22

SAVE THE HUMANS

NUCLEAR FREEZE RALLY, 1982

Activists walk to New York's Central Park on June 12, 1982. Their sign reads "Freeze the arms race."

One million people gather in New York City to call for international peace and an end to nuclear weapons.

Almost forty years after the United States dropped nuclear bombs on Japan at the end of World War II, the world was poised on the brink of nuclear annihilation.

The two global superpowers, the Soviet Union and the United States, were locked in a standoff known as the Cold War. Both countries were in an arms race to see which one could have the most and biggest bombs. Fear and paranoia about nuclear war coming at any moment were widespread. The nightly news covered every detail of nuclear buildup and aggression between the two countries.

An overhead view of the Three Mile Island nuclear plant

Schoolchildren were taught how to "duck and cover" under their desks in case of an attack. The government urged parents to locate or build nuclear fallout shelters, filled with at least a month's worth of food to survive the aftereffects of such an attack.

A lively antinuclear movement was active as well. The Committee for Non-Violent Action formed in 1957 to protest nuclear weapons and war. And in 1961 a group of activists led by outspoken pacifist Bradford Lyttle walked from San Francisco to Moscow to demonstrate unity between the people of the US and the Soviet Union. From these beginnings, the antinuclear movement grew into a global network that also protested the use of nuclear power to generate electricity.

Supporters of nuclear power argued that it was cleaner than oil or gas in terms of pollution. Environmentalists objected to nuclear testing that destroyed landscapes, created toxic waste, and sent harmful radiation into the air. Accidents at nuclear power plants and other nuclear-related facilities happened regularly, causing painful deaths and making certain areas uninhabitable for years.

One 1979 nuclear accident in Pennsylvania, known as the Three Mile Island disaster, struck particular fear about nuclear weapons and plants throughout the country. A stuck valve led to a partial meltdown of the Three Mile Island Nuclear Generating Station's nuclear core, causing the release of dangerous clouds of radiation in the most significant US nuclear accident to date. Although new safety regulations for nuclear plants were announced, the disaster renewed opposition to nuclear weapons and energy.

MARCHING AGAINST ARMS

On June 12, 1982, an estimated one million people filled New York City's Central Park to protest. It was believed to be the world's largest peace rally to date, even larger than the rallies against the Vietnam War. The aim of this nuclear freeze rally was to halt nuclear weapons production and nuclear power plant construction and end the arms race. The rally reflected the antinuclear movement's global appeal. As the *New York Times* reported,

> The vast parade and rally, organized by a coalition of peace groups, brought together pacifists and anarchists, children and Buddhist monks, Roman Catholic bishops and Communist Party leaders, university students and union members. There were delegations from Vermont and Montana, Bangladesh and Zambia, and from many other places. The smiling, hand-clapping line of marchers was more than three miles [5 km] long, and the participants carried placards in dozens of languages.

The rally had a festive atmosphere. A lighthearted and communal break from constant nuclear anxiety, it celebrated the movement's long history of protest. Singers Joan Baez, Bruce Springsteen, Linda Ronstadt, Jackson Browne, and Gary U.S. Bonds represented different decades of protest music. Graffiti artist Keith Haring designed lively posters for the event that featured his trademark "radiant baby," a reference to nuclear radiation. Other posters played with classic symbols such as the dove and the peace sign. Protest signs read "Choose Life," "Freeze or Burn," and "Save the Humans."

During the demonstration, President Ronald Reagan, then in the first term of his presidency, derided the protesters, questioning their patriotism and even suggesting they were spies. His policy was one of macho aggression against the Soviet Union. But he made a surprising turnabout in his second term. His administration launched arms control talks with the Soviet Union, aiming to freeze weapons production and reduce the number in the US arsenal.

Along with Soviet general secretary Mikhail Gorbachev, Reagan proclaimed that "a nuclear war cannot be won and should never be fought." The two promised to eliminate nuclear weapons stationed in Europe and even worked on a plan to abolish all nuclear arms by the year 2000. That plan was left unfinished, but when the Soviet Union dissolved in 1991, the conversation turned from "How many nuclear weapons are needed?" to "How do we prevent a nuclear standoff of this scale from happening again?"

WHERE DID THE PEACE SYMBOL COME FROM?

It's most often equated with the fashionable California hippie culture of the 1960s, sewn onto pockets of bell-bottom jeans, painted on the sides of Volkswagen vans, and waved on giant flags. But the iconic peace symbol—a circle with what looks like a bent fork inside it—was created for a very specific purpose: to symbolize the nuclear disarmament movement.

Designed by Gerald Holtom in 1958 for the British Campaign for Nuclear Disarmament, the symbol combines two letters (*N* and *D* for nuclear disarmament) from the alphabet of semaphore, a visual language used to communicate between ships, often signaling distress. Holtom, a professional designer and conscientious objector who had spent World War II working on an English farm, was in a state of distress himself when he was asked to design signs for a 52-mile (84 km) antinuclear march from London to an atomic weapons research facility. The peace symbol had a double meaning for him.

"I was in despair. Deep despair," about the state of the world, Holtom wrote in a letter to the editor of *Peace News* magazine. "I drew myself: the representative of an individual in despair, with hands palm outstretched outwards and downwards in the manner of [a prisoner] before the firing squad. I formalized the drawing into a line and put a circle round it. It was ridiculous at first and such a puny thing." Holtom made a little button of the symbol to wear on his jacket but totally forgot about it until someone pointed out how cool it looked. That gave him the confidence to present it as the new logo of the antinuclear movement, which quickly adopted it. It became a universal symbol of peace.

CHAPTER 23

OUT AND PROUD FOR LGBTQ RIGHTS

SECOND MARCH ON WASHINGTON FOR LESBIAN, GAY, AND BI EQUAL RIGHTS AND LIBERATION, 1987

Activists explore the first public display of the AIDS Memorial Quilt.

A landmark gathering energizes a national movement in a time of fear and mourning.

Many LGBTQ people felt anxious and angry in 1987. AIDS had killed thousands of people, mostly gay men and people of color, since the disease was first reported in the US in 1981. Scientists had discovered that one way of spreading AIDS was through sexual contact. Because of prejudice, the federal government had offered very few resources for research on how to stop it or education about how it was spread. President Ronald Reagan didn't mention the disease until 1985, and his press secretary had even been recorded making jokes about it.

Conservative Christian groups, with connections in the government, used the disease to paint LGBTQ people as evil, deserving the punishment of AIDS. Also in 1987, the Supreme Court upheld a law that made gay sex illegal, even between two consenting adults in their own home. Some people debated about whether gay people should be rounded up and quarantined from the general population. LGBTQ people feared for their freedom as AIDS continued to take lives.

Instead of going back into hiding, as many gay people had felt forced to do before the 1969 Stonewall Riots, LGBTQ activists decided to do the opposite. They staged a march and six-day rally that drew two hundred thousand people to demand funding for AIDS research and legislation of gay rights. The March on Washington for Lesbian, Gay, and Bi Equal Rights and Liberation in October 1987 attracted national media attention and participants from around the country. Rainbow flags waved alongside US flags throughout the crowd, acts of civil disobedience blocked the Supreme Court steps, and contingents of chanting people in wheelchairs—who were ill with AIDS—led the march.

This wasn't the first major action for gay rights in Washington, DC. One in 1979 had mobilized about eighty thousand people, forming a national movement from previously isolated, local protests. During that event, marchers demanded that Congress pass a comprehensive gay and lesbian rights bill, repeal all antigay laws, ban discrimination in hiring for jobs and the military, and find ways to protect gay and lesbian youth from bullying and harassment.

The demands of the marchers in 1987 weren't much different. They added calls for federal funding for AIDS research, an end to racism, and legal recognition of same-sex relationships—an effort that would lead to the legalization of same-sex marriage almost thirty years later. (The rally included a mass gay wedding service, full of brides and grooms of every gender.) But the demonstration showed how much the movement for gay rights had grown in just a few years. Civil rights leader Cesar Chavez and celebrity Whoopi Goldberg were among those leading the march. Prominent politicians including congressional representative Nancy Pelosi and groundbreaking Black presidential candidate Jesse Jackson participated.

The grassroots activist organization AIDS Coalition to Unleash Power (ACT-UP) inspired many with its call to openly confront bigotry and homophobia in the search for an AIDS cure. LGBTQ people who had felt uncomfortable about who they were found support and validation. And the march and rally provided an opportunity to comfort the sick, exchange the latest news about AIDS research, and mourn with others. The massive AIDS Memorial Quilt, displayed for the first time, commemorated those who had died from the disease.

"We are here today to show America and the world that the gay movement is larger, stronger and more diverse than ever," said participant Buffy Dunker, an eighty-two-year-old grandmother who had recently announced she was gay. The march called attention to the AIDS crisis, and the word *gay*—previously considered a dirty word in most of the country—was spoken aloud on national news stations. Reagan began mentioning AIDS in speeches, and some funding was granted to research it. Another large march followed in 1993, drawing one million participants and building momentum to help elect President Bill Clinton, who promised major reforms in the way government treated gay people.

Out and Proud for LGBTQ Rights

A RAINBOW FLAG FOR PRIDE

How did the rainbow become the symbol of the LGBTQ community? Ever since the Stonewall Riots, gay people had gathered every year to commemorate the anniversary of that first major gay uprising. With picnics in parks and public rallies, they celebrated what became known as Gay Freedom Day. Two cities, Chicago and Los Angeles, also held small marches for gay civil rights.

These first marches were very quiet. Soon, however, other cities started hosting their own marches, combining celebrations of gay identity with determined political purpose. These Pride parades became famous for brightly decorated floats and outspoken community contingents, but something seemed to be missing—an instantly recognizable symbol that would stand for the gay community. In 1977 San Francisco artist Gilbert Baker had a vision to design something that represented "the dawn of a new gay consciousness and freedom."

The original US flag of thirteen stars and thirteen stripes, which hung everywhere for the country's 1976 bicentennial anniversary celebrations, inspired Baker. He also took inspiration from the gay nightclubs and parties he went to, which combined all different kinds of people on the dance floor. So Baker fashioned a rainbow flag that reflected the diversity and values of the gay community as it fought for its own liberty.

The flag consists of different-colored stripes, each representing a specific meaning, from spirit (violet) to healing (orange) and life (red). The flag flew at the 1978 Pride parades and was an immediate hit. The rainbow graces everything from bracelets to tattoos, representing LGBTQ Pride.

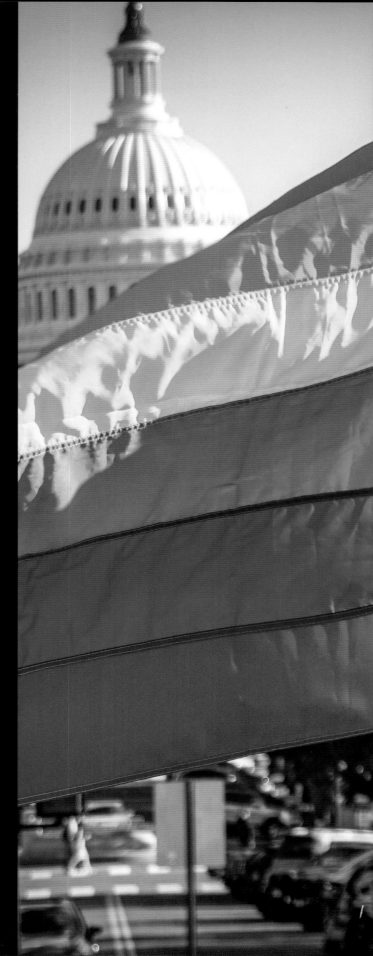

AN AIDS QUILT FOR MOURNING

Baker's friend Cleve Jones, a writer and activist, produced another major symbol of the LGBTQ community (and beyond). The AIDS Memorial Quilt was a colorful commemoration of those lost to the disease.

After gay politician Harvey Milk was assassinated in 1978 in San Francisco, Jones led annual candlelight processions to honor his gay rights legacy. While planning the procession in 1985, Jones learned that more than one thousand San Franciscans had died of AIDS. He asked participants to write the names of people they had lost on signs and walk with them. At the end of the procession, to protest the government's inaction on the disease, Jones and others climbed ladders and taped the signs on the wall of the San Francisco Federal Building.

Jones noticed that the resulting display looked like a quilt. He realized that an actual quilt, comprised of handmade panels representing each person who died, would be a compelling symbol—using a traditional art such as quilting would help more people relate to the disease. Jones fashioned a prototype quilt panel, dedicated to his friend Marvin Feldman, and started the NAMES Project Foundation to help others craft and display their own, connecting each person's panel into one big visual statement.

The response was overwhelming. The first major public display of the quilt, on the National Mall during the 1987 March on Washington, contained almost two thousand panels and covered an area as big as a football field. Each panel contained a name of someone who had died and representations of their personality: sports team logos, musical notes, spiritual symbols, favorite sayings, and even the person's own clothing or art. Half a million people visited its first showing.

Over the next decades, the quilt grew too big to display as one quilt. It contains more than forty-eight thousand individual panels. The striking visual display has toured the country in sections many times to call attention to the AIDS crisis.

ACT-UP AGAINST AIDS

ACT-UP is an international political action group, formed in New York City in 1987, that works to end the AIDS epidemic through civil disobedience and other forms of outreach. Adopting as its symbol the pink triangle, which homosexuals were forced to wear in Nazi Germany, and slogans such as "Silence Equals Death," and "ACT-UP! Fight Back! Fight AIDS!" the organization heralded a new kind of gay activism: radical, unafraid, and controversial.

In its early years, ACT-UP members drew public attention to the AIDS crisis with innovative demonstrations and "zaps" (quick protests). These included blocking Wall Street and chaining themselves to the balcony of the New York Stock Exchange to protest high drug prices, seizing and shutting down the Food and Drug Administration Building, and holding huge die-ins where they lay down and blocked the street, representing all the people who had died of AIDS. ACT-UP helped to develop and distribute lifesaving medication for people who have HIV, the virus that causes AIDS.

People with AIDS and their supporters, some wearing pink triangles, protest in Washington, DC, as part of the 1987 march for lesbian, gay, and bisexual rights.

Harvey Milk sits in front of the camera shop he owned in the Castro neighborhood of San Francisco.

THE LEGACY OF HARVEY MILK

The Stonewall Riots famously launched the contemporary gay rights movement. But fiery politician Harvey Milk became the face of the political struggle for equality, and his legacy directly inspired actions such as the March on Washington.

A navy officer from New York who moved to San Francisco, Milk became the first openly gay politician elected to office in California when he became a city supervisor in 1977. Influenced by the anti-war counterculture movement of the 1960s, Milk was an outspoken advocate of gay liberation who fought for LGBTQ people's rights to teach in public schools and organize for better working conditions. He became a martyr of the gay rights struggle when he was assassinated in 1978, along with San Francisco's mayor, by another city supervisor who held homophobic views. Milk's campaign slogan "You gotta give 'em hope" inspired generations of gay rights activists.

CHAPTER 24

THE BATTLE IN SEATTLE

SEATTLE WTO PROTESTS, 1999

Police officers line up around the Seattle convention center in preparation for protests against the World Trade Organization summit

A protest against global economic inequality and corporate power turns violent.

It was one year before the dawn of a new millennium, and young activists were questioning globalization. Because of the internet, the world was becoming more connected than ever, and people around the world were sharing music, fashion, culture, and knowledge. Corporations that operated on a global scale were connecting people and growing bigger too. To activists, it seemed as though these corporations often had more power and influence than governments over peoples' lives.

Recent free trade agreements between countries, including ones supported by President Bill Clinton, helped bring jobs to poorer parts of the world and cheaper goods to stores. But they also dissolved a lot of workers' rights and environmental regulations that kept global corporations in check. When industries relocated to parts of the world where it was cheaper to operate, US workers lost their jobs. Unemployment skyrocketed in cities that once made cars or manufactured steel products.

Across the globe, income inequality rose, as company owners and investors reaped the rewards of global markets without sharing profits with their workers or putting money back into local communities. As pollution, environmental disasters, and reports of slavelike labor conditions appeared to increase, it felt as if the world was dividing into the rich elite and everybody else.

The World Trade Organization (WTO)—the largest economic organization in the world—was set up in 1994 to regulate negotiations and treaties among countries dealing with global trade. In its fifth year, the WTO chose Seattle, Washington, for the location of its annual members' summit. Seattle is an important global port, more dependent on international trade than most of the country. The city had seen its share of labor struggles throughout its history, including a famous eighty-three-day strike in 1934, which shut down the port and helped create the powerful International Longshore and Warehouse Union.

Yet Seattle in the 1990s was an odd choice for the summit. The city had become an emblem of stylish resistance and anti-capitalist sentiment. Some considered it the center of alternative culture, as the birthplace of grunge music and fashion statements that challenged the US culture of consumerism (until eventually that culture itself became packaged for mainstream consumption). That the organizers overlooked or ignored this cultural shift showed how out of touch they were.

Frustrated activists from across the country and beyond decided to target the WTO summit, to protest its lack of transparency, accountability, and response to the criticisms about globalization. Police and demonstrators clashed violently for five days in what became known as the Battle in Seattle.

Protesters block doors to try to stop WTO delegates from entering the Seattle summit.

THE BATTLE

As the WTO summit began on November 28, protest groups mobilized in organized marches and direct actions. According to one newspaper, "The organizers were a hodgepodge of groups—unions worried about competition from cheap foreign labor, environmentalists worried about the outsourcing of polluting activities, consumer protection groups worried about unsafe imports, labor rights groups worried about bad working conditions in other countries, and leftists of various stripes simply venting their anger at capitalism."

At first, the protests were peaceful, with chanting, sit-ins, and street theater. Ten thousand demonstrators surrounded the downtown convention center and prevented the opening ceremonies. They locked themselves together with metal pipes so they would be harder to arrest and remove. Police overreacted to the relatively tame protests, using pepper spray, tear gas, and rubber bullets on the nonviolent participants.

Meanwhile, twenty-five thousand marchers set out in colorful and spirited contingents to join the downtown protesters from nearby Memorial Stadium. Dozens of environmentalists dressed as turtles and frogs waved banners that read, "Defend our forests, clearcut the WTO." Huge puppets loomed over the crowd, representing silenced indigenous people from around the world, whose homes were threatened by harmful environmental and human rights policies. The Grim Reaper—death—symbolized the fate of the workers' rights.

As the march moved downtown, a few hundred masked anarchists and other political radicals, using destructive "black bloc" tactics of confrontation, broke off and smashed the windows of Starbucks, Nike, Nordstrom, and other global-brand stores. Authorities declared the protest a riot and attacked the marchers.

The next few days descended into chaos. Seattle's mayor imposed a curfew and called in the National Guard. Gas masks, worn to protect protesters from tear gas, were declared illegal, and authorities created a fifty-block "no-protest zone" in the business district. Protesters reacted with more civil disobedience and sit-ins to protest police brutality. Some broke the curfew, smashed more windows, and lit trash cans on fire. Five hundred demonstrators were arrested in one day.

The cycle of protest and crackdown continued until December 3, when the WTO canceled the rest of the summit. The city faced millions of dollars in damage and lawsuits from protesters

A NEW TOOL: THE INTERNET

The WTO protests were among the first major demonstrations to use the power of the internet to organize and amplify the protesters' message. While social media was still a few years in the future, Google had just launched, making it easier to search the web and find events and organizations. Protesters shared information on virtual bulletin boards, in chat rooms, and by group emails.

During the protests, Seattle's Independent Media Center streamed live audio reports and posted video clips. An international internet activist group based in Britain, the Electrohippies Collective organized a "virtual sit-in" of the WTO website. The goal was to have so many people visit the website that it overloaded and shut down. More than four hundred thousand people participated. Actions such as these led to the rise of hacktivism—online protests that included hacking and vandalizing websites for political purposes.

who claimed their civil rights had been violated. Although images of peaceful protesters being teargassed and dragged away shocked the country, those of black-masked anarchists smashing windows shocked people even more, and police units around the country began to arm themselves more heavily against future protests, with military-grade armor and weapons. However, millions of people heard the term *anti-globalization* through coverage of the conflict, and some corporations reexamined how they operated.

The Battle in Seattle

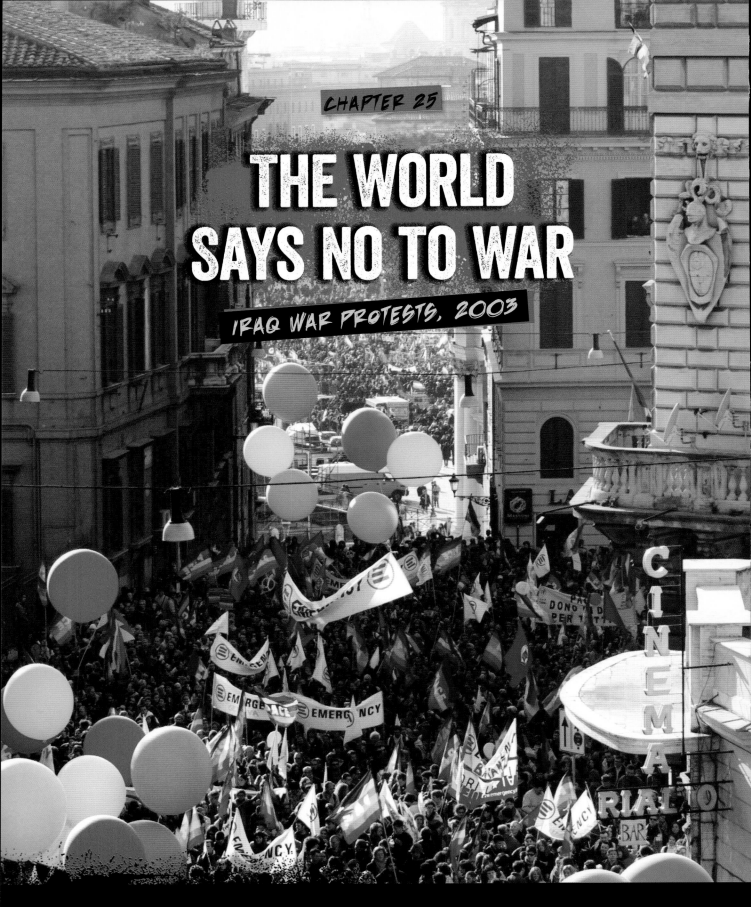

CHAPTER 25

THE WORLD SAYS NO TO WAR

IRAQ WAR PROTESTS, 2003

Iraq War protesters gather in Venezia Square in Rome, Italy.

In the largest coordinated global protests in history, the world rejects another military invasion.

The horrific attacks of September 11, 2001, on New York's World Trade Center and the Pentagon near Washington, DC, killed almost three thousand people and stunned the world. In retaliation, President George W. Bush ordered the invasion of Afghanistan, where the attack's mastermind, Osama bin Laden, and the al-Qaeda terrorist organization were being shielded by the Taliban, a fundamentalist religious group that controlled the country.

The Bush administration then aggressively pushed for invading Iraq and toppling its leader, Saddam Hussein—even though there was no known connection between the country and the 9/11 attacks. The anger and uncertainty of the moment, as well as a wave of anti-Arab racism, helped build momentum for the invasion among US allies. Despite the outcry from millions of citizens that attacking an uninvolved country was unfair, the invasion of Iraq seemed inevitable. The only choice for those who opposed the war was to take to the streets.

On February 15, 2003, young students, veterans, suburban parents, aging hippies, political radicals, elders in wheelchairs, and others poured out in cities around the world, frustrated that their governments weren't responding to their objections. Protest signs in many languages read "Impeach Bush" and "No blood for oil," a reference to Iraq's resources. Chants of "Not in our name" rang out.

Time magazine editor Ishaan Tharoor was one of the protesters in New York City. As word of the scale of other protests seeped in, a feeling of solidarity spread among the demonstrators. Tharoor tallied the global turnout:

> Roughly ten million to fifteen million people (estimates vary widely)
> assembled and marched in more than six hundred cities: as many
> as three million flooded the streets of Rome; more than a million
> massed in London and Barcelona. . . . From Auckland to Vancouver—
> and everywhere in between—tens of thousands came out, joining
> their voices in one simple, global message: no to the Iraq war.

To those on the streets, it felt as though the anti-war spirit of the 1960s had reignited, and "people power" would prevent the invasion. As the *New York Times* put it, "There may still be two superpowers on the planet: the United States and world public opinion."

However, most leaders, Bush included, simply ignored the protests. On March 17, a coalition of countries led by the US launched the invasion. Protesters watched in dismay as newscasters

About two hundred thousand protesters gathered to protest the Iraq War in San Francisco.

celebrated the massive "shock and awe" bombing of the capital, Baghdad. Although Saddam Hussein was eventually captured and executed, the war, which the Bush administration had promised would be swift, ground on for eight more years.

Many more protests occurred throughout those years, but no matter how massive the outcry, things didn't change. Once the United States and its international partners got involved in Iraq, it became impossible to pull out quickly without causing even more damage. The war was described as a quagmire. More than four hundred thousand people were killed, most of them unarmed civilians.

Some demonstrators, looking back, felt they had failed. "I remember at the time everyone saying, 'The baby-boomers sat around and smoked pot, our generation is different—we're going to do something,'" recalled Ed Caldecott, who was seventeen when he joined the London protests. "I was studying the Spanish civil war and in this naive way we thought we were entering one of those big moments, and we weren't. We just felt so betrayed."

Other demonstrators took comfort in the fact that at least they had done something to publicly register their anger at the war—especially years later, when even some of the biggest supporters of the invasion acknowledged it had been a mistake.

"I was just proud to stand with all those people," said Sofia Fenner, a Seattle high school senior at the time. "Proud that we as dissenting Americans were not staying home while what seemed like the whole world took up our cause."

POP GOES THE PROTEST

Like the Vietnam War and its counterculture, the Iraq War (2003–2011) trickled into most aspects of US life. The army chic of clothing designs, televised drill-team dance routines, and the popularity of driving Hummer trucks, which were specifically designed for army use, showed how much US culture had been militarized. Veterans began to show up on reality series and talk shows dealing with aftereffects of deployment, including post-traumatic stress disorder and addiction. Popular video games such as Call of Duty and Prince of Persia were set in Iraq. Politicians and public figures wore little US flag pins on their lapels and jackets or faced accusations of being unpatriotic.

Protest music and culture were not as vibrant and all-encompassing as in the 1960s, but anti-war efforts did make an impact. When hit country act the Dixie Chicks criticized Bush on the eve of the war, they faced death threats and a financially damaging boycott—former fans even ran a bulldozer over a pile of their CDs. Big musical artists such as Madonna, Bruce Springsteen, Eminem, OutKast, Radiohead, and more made statements against the war in music or videos. None, however, provided an anti-war anthem to rival John Lennon's 1969 "Give Peace a Chance" or Marvin Gaye's 1971 "What's Going On?"

As the war numbingly went on, even late-night talk show hosts and comedians such as Jon Stewart, who were among the sharpest public critics of Bush, began to give less coverage to those topics. Instead, they shined their political spotlight on a contender for the 2008 presidential election, Barack Obama, whose campaign slogan "Hope" gave the anti-war protests a new catchphrase.

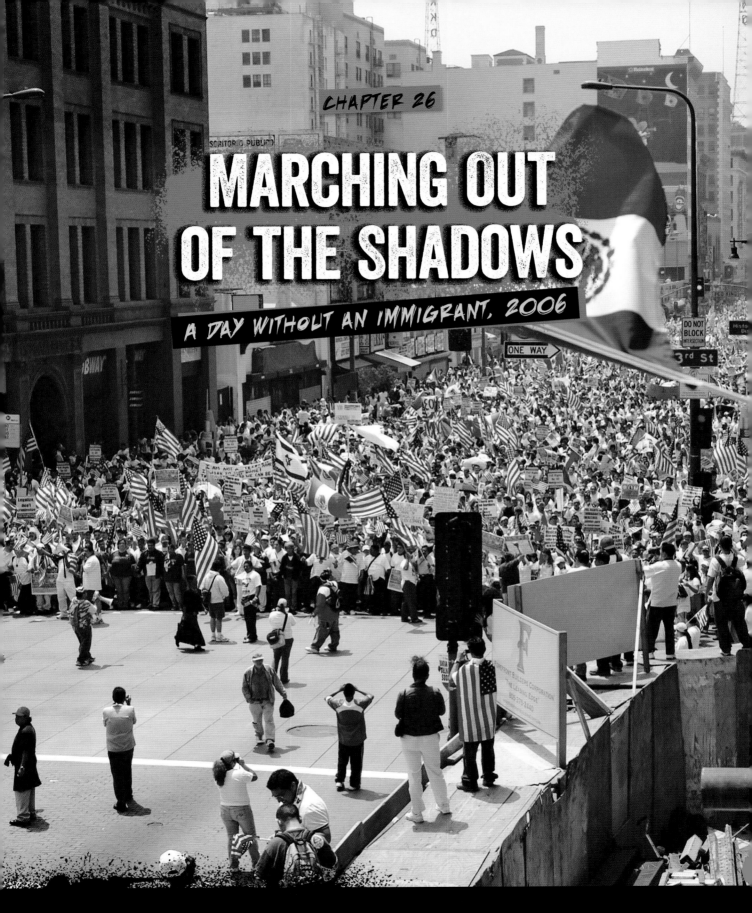

CHAPTER 26

MARCHING OUT OF THE SHADOWS

A DAY WITHOUT AN IMMIGRANT, 2006

Immigrants in Los Angeles gather for La Gran Marcha (the big march) in May 2006.

A silent population shows its value with a nationwide strike and weeks of action.

Marchers in Chicago waved Mexican and US flags, carrying signs that read, "We're not terrorists" and "We build your homes." In Los Angeles, protesters crowded around city hall, climbing trees and bus shelters. Demonstrators in New York City unfurled banners that said, "The USA is a nation of immigrants" and "Hoy marchamos, mañana votamos." (Today we march, tomorrow we vote.)

In Denver, a sea of protesters in white shirts chanted "¡Si, se puede!' (Yes, we can!)

Houston, San Diego, Las Vegas . . . Hundreds of thousands of immigrants and supporters demonstrated in cities around the country on May 1, 2006, for immigrants' right and a clearer path to citizenship. They wore white shirts to symbolize peace, a protest tradition connected to the women's suffrage movement. These activists participated in celebratory and determined actions such as La Gran Marcha in Los Angeles, which drew several hundred thousand people.

The May 1 demonstrations were the culmination of weeks of similar protests that had drawn many undocumented workers and their children into the public eye, a risky action they usually avoided because of their immigration status. The May 1 protest, known as the Great American Boycott, or A Day without an Immigrant, was held on International Workers' Day. Its goal was for all immigrant workers to leave their jobs for one day, to demonstrate their importance to the economy and society.

Almost a million immigrants participated in the one-day strike. As the *New York Times* reported, "Stores and restaurants in Los Angeles, Chicago, and New York closed because workers did not show up. . . . Lettuce, tomatoes and grapes went unpicked in fields in California and Arizona, which contribute more than half the nation's produce. . . . Truckers who move 70 percent of the goods in ports in Los Angeles and Long Beach, Calif., did not work. Meatpacking companies closed plants in the Midwest . . . flower and produce markets stood largely and eerily empty."

An estimated eleven million undocumented people lived in the United States at the time. The catalyst for the protests was a bill that had passed in Congress known as the Sensenbrenner Bill, after its sponsor, Republican congressional representative Frank James Sensenbrenner Jr. of Wisconsin. It proposed harsher punishments for undocumented workers and their employers— even making it a crime for US citizens to assist any undocumented immigrants with food, housing, or medical services.

Demonstrators at the Los Angeles airport protest an anti-immigrant Muslim ban enacted by President Donald Trump in 2017.

The bill would have made the path to citizenship, already confusing for many, much harder. As one young protester from Guatemala said, "I crossed a river and came here as an illegal and now I have a green card [residency] and a profession. I want others to have the same opportunity. The way we treat immigrants at the moment isn't just."

The protests around A Day without an Immigrant were notable because they empowered immigrants to speak out for their rights and point out the current system's flaws. It continued the political organizing of the so-called Dreamers, children of undocumented people who came to the United States as minors, and whose citizenship status remained in question. (Another Day without an Immigrant event, with similar goals, took place in 2017.) "People were actually putting themselves on the line," protest organizer Paul Engler said, "risking their jobs, their safety. . . . I can't even describe what it was like to see people mobilize on that scale for immigrant rights. It was incredible."

ANTI-IMMIGRANT ACTIONS IN THE UNITED STATES

Although A Day without an Immigrant was one of the first major demonstrations in support of immigration, prejudice and actions against immigration have dated to the country's beginnings. Even Benjamin Franklin, the founder and early human rights advocate whose father sailed to North America in 1682, wrote of German immigrants, "Those who come hither are generally of the most ignorant Stupid Sort of their own Nation." The Alien and Sedition Acts of 1798, supported by Thomas Jefferson, framed immigrants as potential spies and made deportation easier.

The nativist Know Nothing political party of the 1840s contained rowdy thugs who beat Catholic, Irish, and German immigrants. White workers' fear that Chinese workers were taking all the railroad jobs led to anti-Chinese riots on the West Coast and the passage of the Chinese Exclusion Act in 1882, which would ban them from immigrating for many years. When turmoil around World War I increased the flow of refugees, panic that they might be political radicals led the government to impose immigration quotas for the first time, ending its open-door policy, which had previously allowed vast numbers to come here.

During the Great Depression, when competition for jobs was high, the US government targeted Mexican immigrant workers for roundups and deportation.

In the midst of World War II, the government placed Japanese immigrants and tens of thousands of US citizens in internment camps, fearing that they sympathized with the enemy. A shipload of Jews fleeing Nazi Germany in 1939 was turned back because of anti-Semitism. Many of its passengers died in concentration camps.

In 1954 and 1955, President Dwight Eisenhower's "Operation Wetback," named for a racist slur, was the largest deportation of undocumented workers in US history. The government took up to 1.3 million from their jobs and homes and dumped them across the border into broiling Mexican towns with no connections or possessions.

After 9/11, Muslim American and immigrant communities were subject to raids and travel restrictions. In 2005 an armed group of twelve hundred US citizens calling themselves the Minuteman Project set to monitor the US-Mexico border in Arizona, to protest what they saw as US inaction against immigration. In 2017 President Donald Trump signed the so-called "Muslim ban," which halted most immigration and travel from seven mostly Muslim countries and provoked widespread protest in airports across the country.

CHAPTER 27

REPRESENTATION FOR NO TAXATION

TEA PARTY PROTESTS, 2009

Demonstrators gather around the steps of the state capitol in Sacramento, California, on April 15, 2009.

A conservative protest movement rooted in the American Revolution remakes the Republican Party.

Democratic nominee Barack Obama won the 2008 presidential election in a decisive victory of more than ten million votes, becoming the country's first Black president. He had campaigned on hope and change after the disastrous invasion of Iraq and the worldwide financial crash of 2008 called the Great Recession. Many media figures declared his election the start of a new age of both major political parties working together and the nation healing from a hurtful political divide.

The Tea Party soon challenged this idealistic view. The protest group adopted the language and imagery of the American Revolution to denounce Obama's policy proposals and even his legitimacy as president. The Tea Party expressed popular grievances held by a significant portion of a certain population—conservative, white, and older. The Tea Party brought many people who had never previously demonstrated into the American protest tradition. Its anger and fear often ballooned into surreal and controversial territory.

The primary concern of the Tea Party was the government's financial response to the Great Recession. That included proposing to spend billions of tax dollars to help huge corporations and banks survive—and also supply some relief to those struggling with home mortgages they could no longer afford. Taxation in general had long been a bugbear of conservatives and libertarians (people who advocate for the idea of a free market without any government intervention).

These new activists considered a large federal government and federal taxes to be against the principles of personal independence that the country had been founded on. The Tea Party name references the Boston Tea Party (see chapter 2). And the use of tax money to help those in trouble was considered socialism, an economic system they dreaded.

The Tea Party officially launched on February 19, 2009, during a broadcast about financial news on cable network CNBC. During a clip from the Chicago Mercantile Exchange, correspondent Rick Santelli called people unable to pay their mortgage "losers," claimed that helping them out would "promote bad behavior," and yelled, "This is America! How many of you people want to pay for your neighbor's mortgage . . . who can't pay their bills? President Obama, are you listening? We're thinking of having a Chicago Tea Party in July."

The rant—and the notion of a "Tea Party" protest around Independence Day—fired the imagination of powerful conservative talk show host Glenn Beck, who heartily promoted it.

The Taxpayer March on Washington, in September 2009, was organized by the Tea Party movement.

A savvy network of conservative media outlets including Fox News amplified the idea. Enthusiastic supporters spread news and created affinity groups on the newly popular social media sites Facebook and Twitter. The Tea Party became a reality, expanding throughout the country.

TEA PARTY PROTESTS

Tea Partiers first appeared in significant numbers in several cities on February 27 to protest a $7.9 billion economic relief package called the American Recovery and Reinvestment Act. They held handmade signs calling the act "Porkulus," comparing it to pig fat, and others that read, "Stop stealing from workers to support deadbeats" and "I'll keep my freedom, you can keep the change," referencing Obama's campaign slogan, "Change."

But it wasn't until April 15, Tax Day, that the Tea Party movement came into full flower. Protesters packed town halls, amphitheaters, and parks, from big cities such as Boston to tiny Yakima, Washington, waving signs and sporting colorful outfits. Activists wearing Revolution-era tricorn hats and silk britches rode in on horses. Others dressed in tall Uncle Sam hats and American Indian ceremonial headdresses, and still more dangled tea bags from their eyeglasses and umbrellas. In Washington, DC, some tossed the tea bags onto the White House lawn.

Thomas Jefferson, Betsy Ross, and Benjamin Franklin impersonators were common, as were Don't Tread on Me flags and other mementos of early American rebellion. Speakers exhorted the crowd to stand up against socialism and for personal responsibility, while musicians played drums and fifes, referencing Revolutionary War militia.

Another major protest followed on July 4, Independence Day, with the same fervor. By then, it was obvious that the Tea Party's targets had expanded beyond what it considered unfair taxation and large government. The movement was also protesting attempts to expand health care to more people through government programs, as well as any attempt to pass gun control laws.

Tea Party star Sarah Palin

Critics pointed out that racist signs and those promoting conspiracy theories were showing up. Some claimed that Obama wasn't a US citizen and was therefore an illegitimate president—the so-called birther conspiracy championed by Donald Trump. Others focused on Obama's middle name, Hussein, and claimed he was a secret agent of radical Muslim terrorists trying to destroy the country. Still others portrayed the president as a monkey or used lynching imagery, tapping into racist stereotypes and threats that referenced the backlash to the civil rights movement.

Critics also said that the Tea Party wasn't a true grassroots movement, since conservative billionaires often paid to organize it, a practice called astroturfing. Some claimed that Tea Partiers lacked a sophisticated historical view of the issues they championed, often misinterpreting the thinking of the country's founders regarding taxation and the role of government.

Many conservative politicians and pundits wholeheartedly embraced the movement. The Tea Party's influence helped Republicans retake the House of Representatives in 2010 and brought a more confrontational tone to the party. Former vice presidential candidate Sarah Palin, politician and pundit Michele Bachmann, former Texas congressional representative Dick Armey, and radio host Beck became stars of the Tea Party. By adopting the techniques of 1960s protests, conservatives found a powerful new political tool.

CHAPTER 28

HERE COMES THE 99 PERCENT

OCCUPY WALL STREET, 2011

Occupy Wall Street demonstrators march to police headquarters in New York City in September 2011.

A nationwide phenomenon reflects broad outrage after economic collapse.

What can a protest with no leader and no established goals accomplish? The Occupy movement showed how powerful a spontaneous, undefined protest could be.

The seeds of Occupy had been sown during the global economic collapse of 2008. The Great Recession lasted nearly two years and was devastating for US workers. Almost nine million people lost their jobs, millions more lost their houses, and major corporations and banks shut down. The government spent billions of dollars to save some of those banks and industries—including the Wall Street investment and lending firms that started the crisis. But many felt it did little to help people who lost their jobs and homes.

The effects of the Great Recession lasted for years. Anger grew when none of the people responsible for the collapse went to prison. In fact, some seemed to grow richer. It became popular to think of the world as divided between the wealthiest 1 percent, who had survived the recession with little overall damage, and the 99 percent, who had suffered.

OCCUPY WALL STREET

On June 19, 2011, the provocative magazine *Adbusters* posted a message with a new hashtag on its website. The language called for protesters to express their anger at the Wall Street investment and lending firms that many held responsible for the Great Recession: "#OCCUPYWALLSTREET: Are you ready for a Tahrir moment? / On Sept 17th, flood into lower Manhattan, set up tents, kitchens, peaceful barricades and occupy Wall Street." September 17 was symbolic as the day the United States had adopted the Constitution in 1787.

The magazine's editors were inspired by massive protests in Egypt, where demonstrators had recently occupied Cairo's Tahrir Square, causing the downfall of the country's dictator as part of a general uprising called the Arab Spring. *Indignados* (indignant ones) in Madrid, Spain, also inspired the editors. The demonstrators had occupied the city's main square for months to protest high unemployment and global economic policies.

The *Adbusters* post went viral, and on September 17, hundreds of people poured into the small Zuccotti Park near Wall Street in New York City, to protest the investment and lending firms they held responsible for the Great Recession. But once the protesters got there, they were unsure what to do. They all came from different political ideologies and backgrounds, and there was no clear leader or agenda.

This proved to be a great strength of the movement, as people from all backgrounds put up tents together and moved in. They set up a kitchen, a twenty-four-hour medical clinic, a free library, and other facilities. Over the next two months, they built a tiny egalitarian society in a carnival-like atmosphere, where everyone was an equal leader and decisions required consensus—everyone had to agree on something for it to happen. Occupy made space for participants to express themselves through speeches, art, and street theater.

One well-known performance had dozens of Occupy members dressed as "corporate zombies" shuffling down Wall Street and clutching wads of fake cash. Signs and banners reading "We are the 99 Percent," "People before Profits," and "Up against the Wall Street" flew high. The country became fascinated by the colorful protest, the good humor of the crowd, and the lack of divisive leading figures with specific political agendas. Occupy had opened up a space for frustrated people to simply exist together. Its broad appeal helped the concept spread, and it was instantly replicated in parks and other public spaces around the country.

"Now entering its fourth week, the Wall Street occupation has become a national phenomenon," the *Washington Post* reported. "The president is interested, celebrities are popping by, and

MIC CHECK!

How can a speaker get the attention of a large group of people, especially with no sound system? In Zuccotti Park and other public spaces where electronically amplified sound was forbidden, Occupy protesters used people power, with an ingenious tool called the human microphone.

The human microphone works like this. First, a speaker gets the attention of the people nearby by saying "mic check!" The speaker repeats "mic check!" That signals the crowd to pay attention. Then the speaker says one short phrase or sentence and pauses while surrounding people loudly repeat it. This goes on until the speech is over, naturally amplifying the speaker's words. It's like a game of telephone, except you shout the words instead of whisper them.

pizza shops are adding the OccuPie to their menus. There is even an Occupy video game in development. The movement has spawned hundreds of Occupy locales in a national Occupy Together network. And now there is talk of going global: Occupy the World."

Occupy Wall Street grew and even became a tourist attraction, until it was forcefully cleared by New York police on November 15. The Occupy movement, however, did go global, continuing in different US cities and more than thirty other countries for many more months. It remains important as an experiment in creating an alternative society, free of explicit agendas, to express frustration.

An activist works on art for May Day protests in Zuccotti Park almost a year after the Occupy Wall Street movement began.

BEHIND THE ANONYMOUS MASKS

Developing alongside the Occupy movement—and sharing the roots of its frustration—was the shadowy Anonymous, an equally undefined hacktivist movement that operated mostly online, leaking government documents and hacking corporate websites. When its members appeared in public or in online broadcasts, they sported masks that resembled the face of British folk hero Guy Fawkes, a religious radical who tried to blow up the House of Lords government building in 1605. Anonymous masks continue to show up in protests around the world.

ANGRY PACIFIST

CHAPTER 29

"HANDS UP, DON'T SHOOT"

FERGUSON UPRISING, 2014

Michael Brown Sr. (*wearing "Chosen" shirt*) leads a memorial march in Ferguson in

A community bands together to fight police brutality and demand justice.

The killing of unarmed teenager Michael Brown on August 9, 2014, in Ferguson, Missouri, was one in a series of police shootings of Black people that roiled the Black community that year. A white police officer shot the eighteen-year-old six times and left his body in the middle of a street for over four hours as police investigated.

He joined others recently killed in questionable circumstances. Police had shot John Crawford III, twenty-two, on August 5 while he held a BB gun in an Ohio Walmart. Eric Garner, forty-three, had died on July 17 after the police put him in an illegal chokehold for selling cigarettes on a street in New York City. Soon to join them would be Tamir Rice, twelve, who was shot in Cleveland on November 22 when an officer mistook his toy gun for a weapon.

Other such incidents occurred. Mostly, the police officers involved in the shootings were white. They weren't fired, and often their supervisors placed them on paid leave throughout follow-up investigations. Most were later acquitted.

Police shooting Black men for nonviolent offenses, or killing rather than peacefully subduing them after altercations, wasn't new. What was new was wide use of social media and cell-phone recording, making it easier for bystanders to record and share what they had witnessed, as well as organize around it. Body and dashboard cameras used by police allowed the press and courts to see more evidence of what had happened.

Also new was a Black president who was knowledgeable about the community's history with the police, and who related publicly to the frustration many felt in the wake of the killings. After the 2012 shooting death of seventeen-year-old Trayvon Martin in Florida by neighborhood watch captain George Zimmerman, who was acquitted, Obama called for "a national soul-searching." He went on to say that Martin, as a young Black male, could have been his son or even himself decades earlier.

The killing of Brown two years later enraged people again. Particularly upsetting was the handling of the case. The St. Louis County Police Department held a press conference in which they claimed Brown was killed because he had reached for the officer's gun. The police department refused to release the identity of the officer, however, or other specific details. To outsiders, this seemed like a secretive cover-up of the incident, and getting justice for Brown felt out of reach. A grand jury eventually acquitted Darren Wilson, the white officer who had shot Brown.

"Hands Up, Don't Shoot"

BLACK LIVES MATTER

www.blacklivesmatter.org

Demonstrators in Ferguson mark the one-year anniversary of Michael Brown Jr.'s death.

#BLACKLIVESMATTER

After Trayvon Martin's killer was acquitted, protesters, many wearing hoodies like Martin often wore, took to the streets of more than one hundred cities. Among the familiar protest chants was a new one: "Black lives matter." The phrase and hashtag had been coined by three Black women—Alicia Garza, Opal Tometi, and Patrisse Khan-Cullors. They established Black Lives Matter as "a Black-centered political will and movement building project," and "an affirmation of Black folks' humanity, our contributions to this society, and our resilience in the face of deadly oppression." Black Lives Matter came to national attention during the Ferguson unrest, and its name grew to become a rallying cry during the following years of protests.

FERGUSON PLAYLIST

Since its beginning, hip-hop expressed political feelings and spread news among the Black community. The Ferguson uprising and the Black Lives Matter movement produced some memorable songs by famous rappers, including Beyoncé's "Freedom," Kendrick Lamar's "Alright," Janelle Monáe's "Hell You Talmbout," and Common and John Legend's "Glory." "Sandra's Smile" by Blood Orange memorializes Sandra Bland, who died in jail under suspicious circumstances after a white police officer pulled her over and arrested her, and Prince's "Baltimore" was his response to the death of Freddie Gray, who died of injuries he received while in police custody.

THE UPRISING

News of Brown's shooting and subsequent police silence sparked outrage, and dozens of protesters gathered the next morning outside the Ferguson police department. Brown's father led them in a chant of "We are one," but unrest quickly spread. That night, after a candlelight vigil, more than three hundred police officers were dispatched to answer reports of smashed windows, arson, and looting.

Over the next eleven days, peaceful protests alternated with clashes between demonstrators and police, along with incidents of property damage. Protesters came from around the country to participate in what they saw as an important moment in the continued fight for civil rights. They chanted, "Black lives matter" and "We can't breathe" (a quote from victim Eric Garner's repeated pleas to police, recorded on video), and to journalists in the area, "Tell the truth." A witness to Brown's death said he'd had his hands up and said "Don't shoot" before he died. The FBI later declared this false, but "Hands up, don't shoot" became a protest slogan.

The protest was a media event that often played out like a ritual. Each night a mass of protesters would face off against police in heavy riot gear, with journalists on the sidelines, until something would spark disorder. Many observers were surprised at the amount and types of police weaponry used: tear gas grenades, armored trucks, and padded uniforms. Images of protesters running from grenades and washing tear gas from their eyes with milk emphasized how much the police force had militarized since 9/11.

The protests in Ferguson eventually petered out, but then they expanded to different parts of the country where other police killings had occurred, such as Baltimore and Chicago. "If they would lock the police officer up that shot Mike Brown, none of this would be going on. . . . There's no excuse for it. We want something done," said Mek Mack, a Ferguson resident, during the protests.

Another protest participant, Brittany Packnett, put the events in a wider context when she said, "I think the most significant thing that has changed is that people can see this isn't just about Mike Brown. . . . It is about defending the humanity and the dignity of all people in this country and of people of color in particular."

"Hands Up, Don't Shoot"

CHAPTER 30

CLIMATE PROTESTS HEAT UP

PEOPLE'S CLIMATE MARCH, 2014

Thousands stand up against climate change in Lima, Peru, as part of the People's Climate March.

Sunflowers, giraffes, dinosaurs, and hundreds of thousands of people join an environmental protest.

"This is an invitation, an invitation to come to New York City. An invitation to anyone who'd like to prove to themselves, and to their children, that they give a damn about the biggest crisis our civilization has ever faced," wrote leading environmentalist Bill McKibben in a 2014 article titled "A Call to Arms: An Invitation to Demand Action on Climate Change." McKibben continued,

> My guess is people will come by the tens of thousands, and it will be the largest demonstration yet of human resolve in the face of climate change. Sure, some of it will be exciting—who doesn't like the chance to march and sing and carry a clever sign through the canyons of Manhattan? But this is dead-serious business, a signal moment in the gathering fight of human beings to do something about global warming before it's too late to do anything but watch. You'll tell your grandchildren, assuming we win.

Because climate change affects the world, protests that focus on it are often on a global scale. The United States, however, has been one of the slowest countries to recognize climate change officially as a threat. Indeed, many politicians deny it even exists, even as millions of climate change refugees flee their countries, Arctic ice melts at an unprecedented rate, catastrophic weather events happen more often, animal species rapidly go extinct, and seas continue to rise.

Although the government seemed stalled on climate change, activists and protesters weren't. On September 21, more than three hundred thousand people in New York and hundreds of thousands more around the world—in cities including New Delhi, India; Bogotá, Colombia; and Lagos, Nigeria—answered McKibben's call.

Indigenous peoples marching in New York created this representation of Mother Earth.

EXTINCTION REBELLION

The international group Extinction Rebellion, launched in 2018, has attracted attention to climate change with its bold and energetic protests. On April 15, 2019, it helped stage an international rebellion event, in which the organization closed London bridges, chained themselves to the Canadian prime minister's door, and shut down New York City's Brooklyn Bridge.

Two weeks before that, a dozen Extinction Rebellion activists had stripped and glued themselves to the House of Commons government building in England, drawing attention to the "naked truth" of ecological collapse. Two of them wore gray body paint and elephant masks to indicate that climate change was the unspoken "elephant in the room."

The People's Climate Movement organized the People's Climate March. The movement uses a "compassionate response" to climate change through mass mobilization of the population and connecting people "under the banner of climate, jobs, and justice, and lifting up core priorities of economic and racial justice."

THE MARCH

The New York march used that principle of connection, using themes to join people of similar experience and goals together to increase their visibility. The front of the march, named Frontlines of Crisis, Forefront of Change, included people at the front lines of the immediate effects of climate change (such as indigenous peoples) and those at the forefront of trying to make

Activists in Minneapolis marched in solidarity with the People's Climate March.

a difference (such as environmental justice organizations). Other groups included We Have Solutions (renewable energy and resources) and We Can Build the Future (labor organizations, families, students, and elders).

The protests were almost as picturesque as nature itself. Giant replicas of Noah's Ark and inventive giraffe puppets represented endangered animals. A shimmering metal dinosaur skeleton symbolized destructive fossil fuels. The contingent leading the parade held aloft an entire field's worth of bright paper sunflowers. A Spanish-language group featured feather-bedecked Aztec dancers and pounding drums. A flock of silk kites shaped like elegant cranes soared above the thrumming crowd.

In a rare move for a United Nations leader, Secretary-General Ban Ki-moon joined the protests with former vice president and prominent climate activist Al Gore and conservationist Jane Goodall. A good-humored yet fierce protest squad called the Raging Grannies came out in pinafores and straw hats to sing a few motivational numbers. A street performance pitted Mother Nature against Father Time in a battle for Earth's fate.

The next day, thousands took part in Flood Wall Street, a civil disobedience protest in which the Climate Justice Alliance, a network of environmental action groups, blocked traffic in the Financial District. They wanted to bring attention to the harmful policies of Wall Street corporations, especially toxic pollution for manufacturing, encouraging deforestation, and not obeying other environmental regulations.

After the march, Secretary of State John Kerry said that "there is a long list of important issues before all of us, but the grave threat that climate change poses warrants a prominent position on that list." In spite of this well-attended action and the support of prominent international leaders, the United States has done little to address climate change, especially compared with the rest of the world.

ON THE FRONT LINES: GRETA THUNBERG

In 2018 Greta Thunberg, a fifteen-year-old Swedish girl, began skipping school every Friday to protest by herself outside the Riksdag, the Swedish parliament, drawing attention to the dire need for climate change action. Her actions and the worldwide press she attracted led to an international school strike.

On March 15, 2019, 1.4 million students in 112 countries took Thunberg's cue and skipped school, for climate change protests. Thunberg has become one of the world's leading voices for climate change action. Called the greatest current threat to the fossil fuel industry, she has been nominated for a Nobel Peace Prize.

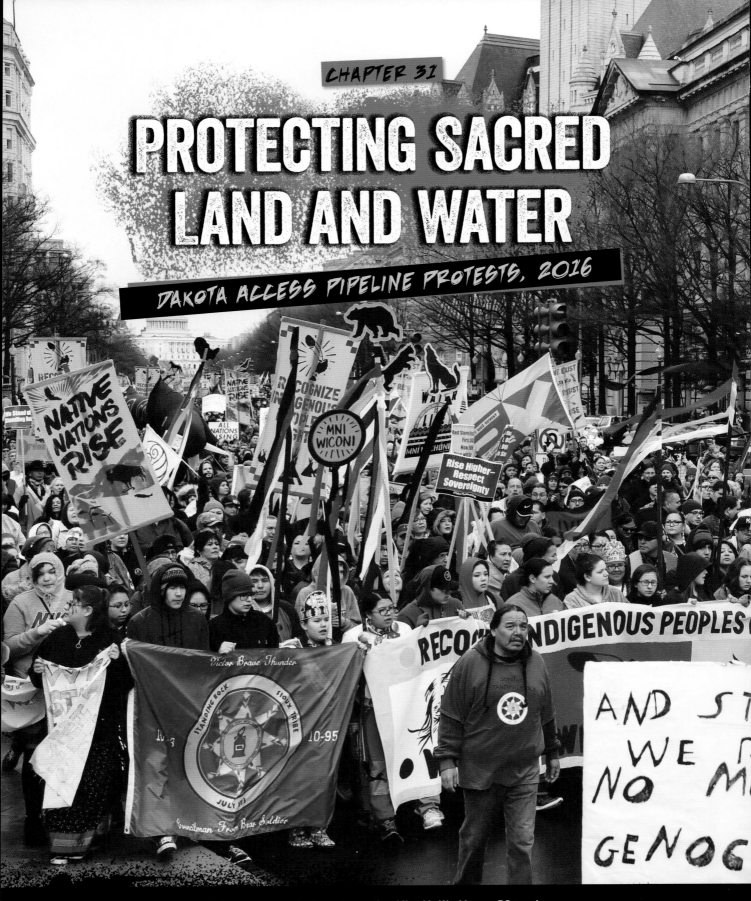

CHAPTER 31

PROTECTING SACRED LAND AND WATER

DAKOTA ACCESS PIPELINE PROTESTS, 2016

Activists gather near the Trump International Hotel in Washington, DC, to raise
their voices for Native nations and against the Dakota Access Pipeline in 2017.

Environmental activism, cultural preservation, and spiritual resistance converge in North Dakota.

It was an ecological protest started by young Sioux girls, mostly through the internet. They were concerned about the damage a giant oil pipeline called the Dakota Access Pipeline (DAPL) would inflict on their home, the Standing Rock Indian Reservation. Especially worrying was how the pipeline might affect the area's water, which the reservation depended on, and the threat it posed to burial grounds held sacred by the Standing Rock Sioux Tribe.

Camps at Standing Rock Indian Reservation, where people traveled to protest the Dakota Access Pipeline

The pipeline, a $3.8 billion project developed by Energy Transfer Partners, a Texas-based company, would stretch more than 1,000 miles (1,600 km) from oil fields in North Dakota to storage sites in southern Illinois. The Sioux said that the pipeline's route under the Missouri River, just a half mile (1 km) from the reservation, could endanger their water supply if it ruptured and spilled oil.

They also said that the pipeline was crossing areas of cultural significance that were under protection of federal law. The Standing Rock Indian Reservation was in a region that had played a big part in the history of protest, including the Wounded Knee Massacre and the Wounded Knee Incident, and DAPL awakened its protest spirit once again.

First, thirteen-year-old Anna Lee Rain Yellowhammer launched a petition on Change.org, urging the Army Corps of Engineers, which was reviewing the pipeline's route, to halt construction. "In Dakota/Lakota [Sioux language] we say 'Mni Wiconi.' Water is life," Rain Yellowhammer wrote in the petition. "Native American people know that water is the first medicine, not just for us, but for all human beings living on this earth." Then she and thirty others started the Standing Rock Kids and kicked off the ReZpect Our Water campaign. The word *reZpect* was a combination of *respect* and *rez*, which is slang for reservation.

Protecting Sacred Land and Water

Then twelve-year-old Tokata Iron Eyes started the #NoDAPL hashtag on Twitter, which along with #NoDakotaAccess and #StandWithStandingRock, quickly went viral. The teens and their friends produced a short, simple video to lay out the issues, and they posted pictures of themselves on Instagram holding signs with the hashtags and a website address. Through their internet savvy and intelligent quotes to the press, they helped the Change.org petition receive more than eight hundred thousand signatures.

It also reached around the world and prompted many people, including many who had never protested before, to come to Standing Rock to oppose the pipeline.

Demonstrators in Los Angeles protest a presidential order fast-tracking the oil pipeline in February 2017.

THE PROTEST

When the Army Corps of Engineers approved the pipeline, the tribe sued the government to stop its construction. Those opposed to the pipeline, including members of other tribes, camped at its site. LaDonna Brave Bull Allard, a Standing Rock Sioux elder, established the spacious Sacred Stone Camp. It was a cultural center and hub of spiritual practice and efforts to preserve native sovereignty.

At first, three thousand people lived at Sacred Stone, but as more attention came to the struggle, eventually fifteen thousand lived there. Non-Indian activists joined Indian ones from around the country to share in ceremony and resistance. Twenty-seven-year-old chef and Rosebud Sioux tribe member Nantinki Young set up a kitchen, saying, "As soon as I heard this was happening, I wanted to make sure that I was here. I felt like my heart was here. It's not our tribe, I'm not from here, but we're all Native Americans, and we all stand together. At first, it was just like a little campsite. Now it's turned into a community."

A statement from the United Nations supported the Standing Rock protesters—or, as they called themselves, Water Protectors. Activists chained themselves to the heavy construction equipment used for the pipeline. Protesters chanted, "Can't drink oil, keep it in the soil!" Banners read, "I can live without oil but I can't live without water."

President Obama ordered an environmental review of the pipeline's path. The protesters were considered trespassers, as they had camped on private property. Some were arrested—

actor Shailene Woodley live-streamed her arrest on Facebook. When camp members went to pray at a nearby creek, police pepper-sprayed and shot rubber bullets at them. Obama urged police restraint, but the arrested protesters claimed they were stripped, kept in dog kennels, and had numbers written on them, an echo of Nazi concentration camps during the Holocaust.

But the protesters won some victories. The pipeline was at first put on hold, and then several safety restrictions were added. The Sacred Stone Camp dug in for a long North Dakota winter, fearing more raids but staying together and hoping for a permanent block or rerouting of the pipeline. In January 2017, however, newly elected president Donald Trump ordered that the pipeline be built and that all public comment and environmental review end. Tribal leaders vowed to keep up resistance by other means.

TREES TO OCEANS: NOTABLE ECO-ACTIVISM TACTICS

Besides blocking construction sites with camps, here are some other notable ways environmentalists have taken action:

Tree sitting. Moving into trees is one way to keep loggers from cutting them down (sometimes). In 1999 Julia "Butterfly" Hill broke records by living in a 180-foot (55 m), six-hundred-year-old California redwood tree called Luna for 738 days. Her action saved Luna.

Radical interventions. These can include breaking into farms and laboratories to free captive animals or protesters chaining themselves to machinery and sabotaging equipment to prevent environmental harm. The Sea Shepherd Conservation Society protects whales and other ocean life by using a fleet of ships to block or damage whaling and fishing ships.

Nude bike rides. Once a year for the World Naked Bike Ride, thousands of participants in more than seventy cities shed their clothes and ride their bikes to bring attention to climate change and oil dependency. The clothing-optional, human-powered transport protest certainly catches attention.

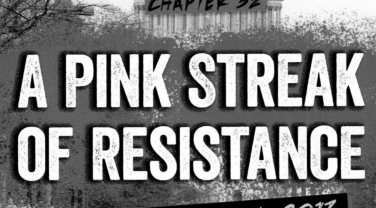

A PINK STREAK OF RESISTANCE

THE WOMEN'S MARCH, 2017

Participants in the Women's March in Washington, DC, numbered around five hundred thousand

After a controversial election, women and supporters take to the streets in record numbers.

In the 2016 presidential election, Hillary Clinton, the first woman representing a major political party to run for president, won the popular vote by almost three million ballots. But her rival, Donald Trump, won the electoral college vote, so he won the presidency.

The election was immediately met with disappointment from people who had hoped the United States would elect its first female president. Trump's aggressive language toward women and minorities during his election campaign added to the anger. Many women felt especially upset by Trump since the release of the so-called *Access Hollywood* tape, a recording from backstage at a TV show in which he used crude and misogynistic language to brag about sexual assault.

The day after the election, Hawaiian lawyer and educator Teresa Shook posted to Facebook, asking friends if they wanted to march together on Inauguration Day. An event page received hundreds of thousands of responses. A movement was born. The main event was supposed to be in Washington, DC, but other cities joined in too, as far away as Osaka, Japan, and Nairobi, Kenya. Many women felt ready to channel their frustration. (Not all women were angry, however. A significant portion of white women had voted for Trump and helped him win.)

Shook said her original intent was to "show the capacity of human beings to stand in solidarity and love against the hateful rhetoric that had become a part of the political landscape in the US and around the world. I wanted us to prove that the majority of us are decent people who want a world that is fair, just and inclusive of women and all people."

The response was so great that the march needed some professional planning, and four people from diverse backgrounds were the organization's cochairs: Tamika D. Mallory, Carmen Perez, Bob Bland, and Linda Sarsour. As the event expanded, national groups including the American Civil Liberties Union (ACLU), Amnesty International, Planned Parenthood, GLAAD, and the Muslim Women's Alliance signed on.

THE WOMEN'S MARCH

On January 21, somewhere between three and five million people marched around the country. Although the march centered on women and their concerns, it included topics from LGBTQ rights to immigration reform. Generations of women marched together, from ninety-year-olds in wheelchairs to nine-month-olds in strollers. The color theme was hot pink, and the streets radiated with the intensity of the hue and the marchers' determined energy.

A Pink Streak of Resistance

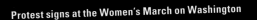

Protest signs at the Women's March on Washington

In Washington, DC, a rally on the National Mall featured performances and speeches by musician and artist Yoko Ono, singer Miley Cyrus, educator Angela Davis, singer Janelle Monáe, and many more. (A nearby "peace ball," held as a protest alternative to the traditional inauguration ball, featured singer Solange Knowles, actor Ellen Page, and author Alice Walker.)

Marchers labeled themselves the Resistance. Signs read, "Women's rights are human rights," "Who Run the World? Girls" (after the Beyoncé song), "Nasty women make history" (referring to a term Trump used to insult Clinton), and "Fempire strikes back" (a *Star Wars* reference).

"I feel that in the face of this current political climate, it is vital that we all make it our mission to get really, really personal," said actor Scarlett Johansson at the DC rally. "President Trump, I did not vote for you. I want to be able to support you. But first I ask that you support me. Support my sister. Support my mother. Support my best friend and all of our girlfriends."

Feminist leader Gloria Steinem said, "Make sure you introduce yourselves to each other and decide what we're going to do tomorrow, and tomorrow and tomorrow," she said. "We're never turning back!"

As if to answer Steinem's call, the march even came with a list of action items to help continue the protest's momentum. Called "10 Actions for the First 100 Days," these included writing postcards and forming huddles—smaller groups that could provide support and plan for the next action.

Trump ignored the march, visiting the CIA headquarters and bragging about the size of the crowd at his inauguration speech. But the spectacle of the enormous Women's March stole his media thunder. In 2018 even more people marched, and the Women's March officially became an annual event.

THE PUSSYHAT

During the Women's March, it seemed as though everyone sported the same hat: pink, with little cat ears (*above*). The story behind them began in 2016 when Los Angeles artist Jayna Zweiman was recovering from an injury and looking for something to do. She convinced her friend Krista Suh to take a crochet class with her at a place called the Little Knittery.

In 2017 Suh was heading to the Women's March, but Zweiman's injury kept her home. Suh needed something to keep her head warm, and Zweiman wanted a way for her voice to be heard. They conceived an iconic hat design that would fill both needs, creating a bold visual statement. They envisioned a sea of such hats, in a striking shade of pink.

Aurora Lady of the Little Knittery came up with the pattern from their ideas. The name for it, Pussyhat, was chosen "in part as a protest against vulgar comments Donald Trump made about the freedom he felt to grab women's genitals, to destigmatize the word 'pussy' and transform it into one of empowerment, and to highlight the design of the hat's 'pussycat ears.'" Soon the hat was the must-have item for the annual protest.

CHAPTER 33

WHITE MALE RAGE ERUPTS

UNITE THE RIGHT RALLY, 2017

In Charlottesville, Virginia, white supremacists and counterprotesters gather around a statue of Thomas Jefferson

A white nationalist gathering reveals a violent backlash to the country's growing diversity.

They came to Charlottesville, Virginia, in pressed khaki pants and white polo shirts. Their hair was swept to the side, and their mouths were twisted in rage or smirking with superiority. They carried lit Tiki torches they'd bought at Walmart, echoing the burning torches and crosses of the Ku Klux Klan. They shouted racist slogans, including "Jews will not replace us," "White lives matter" (a response to Black Lives Matter), and "Blood and soil" (an old German Nazi saying that defined Christian white people as the only legitimate citizens of the country).

The white supremacists advanced on the students, making monkey noises and throwing their torches at them.

On the night of Friday, August 11, 2017, a column of about 250 white supremacists, almost all young men, trooped into Nameless Field near the University of Virginia, looking like a cross between the mob of furious townspeople in *Frankenstein* and a Fascist rally from the twentieth century. This big media moment, led by strident neo-Nazi Richard Spencer, would put the alt-right—a conservative movement he had helped put together—on the national stage.

The alt-right, or alternative right, focuses on promoting white identity above any form of diversity, and it rejects advances in civil rights for minorities. The group uses social media and memes, as well as a unique style of dress, to try to appeal to young white people who are angry that the country is getting more diverse. It is "dedicated to the heritage, identity, and future of people of European descent in the United States," and Spencer himself advocates for a "peaceful ethnic cleansing" of the country, which would leave it all white.

As the alt-right members raged, a group of thirty students moved into the park and locked arms around a statue of Thomas Jefferson, who had founded the university. The students, both white and of color, protested the alt-right's presence. The white supremacists advanced on the students, making monkey noises and throwing their torches at them. The two groups scuffled until the police, who had been absent throughout the gathering, intervened.

Friday night's protest was a surprise. The group, along with other white supremacist and neo-Nazi organizations, had a permit for a big demonstration the next day at Emancipation Park.

People pay their respects at a memorial for Heather Heyer, who was killed by a white nationalist in Charlottesville.

Why were they there? It had to do with another statue. Emancipation Park had been called Lee Park, after a statue honoring Confederate general Robert E. Lee.

The previous year, the Lee statue had been removed after public outcry over celebrating such a major participant in the country's racist past. Many other such statues were removed throughout the South in a wave of protest that saw them as harmful. The majority relocated to museums or other appropriate places for historical study and preservation. Several parks where they had stood were renamed.

White nationalists saw this removal as an attack on their cultural heritage and history. Hundreds had come to Charlottesville to gather, protest and, as the rally was called, Unite the Right.

THE RALLY

The next morning, tempers in the city were running hot from the clash the night before. White nationalist groups other than the alt-right included neo-Confederates, neo-Fascists, and Ku Klux Klansmen. They carried banners, clubs, swords, shields, and guns and displayed various racist symbols such as the swastika and the iron cross. Some waved Confederate and Nazi flags. Others wore Nazi and Ku Klux Klan uniforms.

A huge group of counterprotesters came out to meet them. They represented the Black Lives Matter movement, several religious peace and civil rights organizations, and others. Thirty counterprotesting clergy members clasped arms and began singing "This Little Light of Mine" while 20 feet (6 m) away white nationalists screamed back, "Our blood, our soil!" Into this scene

INTO THE STREETS

came a third group: three dozen armed, self-appointed peacekeepers—a local militia whose loaded weapons made everyone nervous.

The white nationalist groups were supposed to march along a strictly prescribed route to get into Emancipation Park. But instead, they overwhelmed other entrances and headed right for the counterprotesters. As the *Washington Post* reported, "With a roar, the marchers charged through the line, swinging sticks, punching and spraying chemicals. Counterprotesters fought back, also swinging sticks, punching and spraying chemicals. Others threw balloons filled with paint or ink at the white nationalists. Everywhere, it seemed violence was exploding. The police did not move to break up the fights."

The scene melted down even more, with various skirmishes breaking out throughout the day, with activists using weapons such as fire extinguishers, flagpoles, lit spray-paint canisters, and blowtorches. The violence kept escalating until white nationalist James Fields Jr. purposefully gunned his car into a crowd of resting protesters, injuring nineteen and killing a young peace activist named Heather Heyer.

After the tragedy, Trump sparked controversy when he said both sides of the conflict had been to blame for the violence. White nationalist demonstrations and spirited counterprotests took place in several other cities over the next year. Several mass shootings that followed Unite the Right were attributed to white nationalist motives.

ANTIFA

Another group that seized the national-conversation after Unite the Right was antifa. Antifa stands for anti-Fascist. The protest movement includes individual groups that oppose fascism and violent right-wing organizations. The movement believes in using direct action, including violence, to stop Fascist groups such as the alt-right. Many regard force as the only way to stop the rise of neo-Nazi groups when the police and government aren't stepping in.

At the Unite the Right rally, antifa members used clubs and dyed liquids against white nationalists. Antifa activists often wear masks to prevent doxing, or the exposure of their personal information online, which leaves them vulnerable to attack by white supremacists. This use of violence and anonymity has caused some Republican officials to consider labeling antifa domestic terrorists.

CHAPTER 34

#ENOUGHISENOUGH

MARCH FOR OUR LIVES, 2018

Activists in Reno, Nevada, join the March for Our Lives protest.

In the wake of a mass school shooting, students organize one of the biggest protests in US history.

February 14, 2018, started as a normal Wednesday at Marjory Stoneman Douglas High School in Parkland, Florida. It was Valentine's Day, and classmates had exchanged carnations over lunch. The tennis team raised money selling hoodies. Some students put down deposits on graduation class rings.

Shortly after two o'clock, an Uber driver dropped off former student Nikolas Cruz outside the school. Armed with a semiautomatic rifle, he entered a building with about nine hundred students inside. He pulled the fire alarm and started shooting indiscriminately as students exited classrooms.

Seventeen students and faculty members died, and seventeen more were injured. Students who knew Cruz called 911 and identified him. But he blended in with students as they ran out. He was later arrested after he went to a nearby mall for a soda.

Mass shootings were becoming more common in the United States, many directly targeting young people. Shooters at Colorado's Columbine High School killed thirteen in 1999. In 2007 a shooter killed thirty-two at Virginia Tech college. Twenty-six, mostly young children, were killed in 2012 at Sandy Hook Elementary in Connecticut. The two years before the Parkland massacre had seen forty-nine killed at Orlando's Pulse nightclub, fifty-eight at an outdoor concert in Las Vegas, and twenty-six at a church in Sutherland Springs, Texas. There were many more.

After each shooting, the country engaged in deeply divisive arguments over whether and how the shooting could have been prevented. Many liberal lawmakers and much of the country's population supported stricter gun control laws. Powerful gun lobbyists and many conservatives

Parkland activists, *left to right*: Alex Wind, Emma González, Cameron Kasky, Jaclyn Corin, and David Hogg

emphasized mental health or lack of armed security as the problem. Arguments erupted over how much the Second Amendment, guaranteeing the right to bear arms, extends to cover contemporary weapons the founders never dreamed of. Not much got decided before the next shooting occurred.

This time, though, Marjory Stoneman Douglas students decided to take a stand. What had been missing in the debates, they felt, were the voices of students who themselves had been victims of gun violence. Several students banded together to form Never Again MSD, a political organization that advocates for more gun control.

The group's goal was to "create a new normal where there's a badge of shame" on politicians accepting donations from gun lobbyists while doing nothing about gun laws, student Cameron Kasky told the press. "You're either with us or against us," he said. "We are losing our lives while the adults are playing around."

Kasky and fellow students Emma González, David Hogg, Alex Wind, Jaclyn Corin, and Sarah Chadwick quickly became media stars, using social media and their press attention to gain momentum for actions against gun violence. Three days after the shooting, González gave a viral speech in which she passionately shouted, "We call B.S." on current gun laws and government inaction.

On March 14, the one-month anniversary of the Parkland shooting, nearly one million students in three thousand schools around the country participated in the Enough! National School Walkout to protest gun violence. That was the prelude to an even bigger action.

"Now is the time to come together, not as Democrats, not as Republicans, but as Americans."

THE MARCH

On March 24, students and their supporters flooded Pennsylvania Avenue in Washington, DC, for the March for Our Lives. Almost nine hundred other cities held similar marches. Two million people turned out for one of the largest protests in US history. Parkland students organized the march with help from celebrities such as George Clooney, Oprah Winfrey, Taylor Swift, Justin Bieber, Harry Styles, Alyssa Milano, and many more.

The protesters had several demands: universal background checks on all gun sales, banning high-volume gun magazines, restoring a ban on assault weapons, and closing the loophole that allows people to buy guns at gun shows without the usual background checks.

Speeches by the Parkland students urged young people to vote when they turned eighteen and to contact their congressional representatives and other lawmakers about gun control, holding them accountable for all their votes and campaign contributions. "Today is the beginning of spring, and tomorrow is the beginning of democracy," Hogg urged from the podium. "Now is

March for Our Lives activists in Saint Paul, Minnesota

the time to come together, not as Democrats, not as Republicans, but as Americans. Americans of the same flesh and blood, that care about one thing and one thing only, and that's the future of this country and the children that are going to lead it," he said.

Like the teenagers who started the Dakota Access Pipeline protests, the Parkland students and March for Our Lives organizers built a strong social media presence. Hashtags #NeverAgain, #EnoughIsEnough and #MarchForOurLives were retweeted by singers Lady Gaga, Ariana Grande, and Miley Cyrus. Snapchat created a special March for Our Lives sticker, and its mapping function was used to track individual marches in cities around the country, streaming live videos from many of them. An advertising agency collaborated with students to create the first Instagram coloring book for March for Our Lives.

After the march, Gonzaléz said she felt hopeful, because "I've met so many people who are ready to engage in our political system, and these are exactly the people we need to engage. People who are devoted to the concept of keeping people safe, focusing on the rights of people who need to be kept in mind, who need to be kept alive. People who are looking out for each other, not just themselves."

HOW TO START A PROTEST OF YOUR OWN

ozens of other fascinating protests occurred throughout our country's history—so many we couldn't possibly fit them in this book.

Those include major actions such as the 1995 Million Man March on Washington, meant to empower Black men and combat racial stereotypes. The antiabortion March for Life is the longest-running protest in the country, started in 1974 after the Supreme Court declared abortion legal. The 2004 protests against the Republican National Convention in New York City brought out a cavalcade of theatrical protest groups, including Billionaires for Bush and Witches Opposing War, who used satire and humor to show dissatisfaction with President George W. Bush.

Many of the protests we've covered have used similar tactics to achieve similar goals. They find ways to unite people through chants, signs, costumes, props, and songs. They draw media attention with striking looks, gimmicks, and messages. And they engage clearly and directly with issues to convince others to join or support them. This book has given you a sense of the visual language that most protests share, as well as an overview of the different kinds of protests used over the past several hundred years.

If you pay attention to the news, dig into social media, or look around your community, you'll find not just issues to protest but protests themselves. Usually, people need an issue to affect them directly—from possibly being drafted into a war to the closing of a local library due to budget cuts—before they consider protesting. But that doesn't mean you can't form an opinion on a subject and support actions taken by others expressing their frustration or sadness.

You may even want to start a protest of your own. While there is no real one-size-fits-all blueprint for protests, here are some tips that can help get you started:

1. **Define a goal.** Although many protests are spontaneous outpourings of emotion, the key to an effective one is to know what you want to achieve, whether it's bringing attention to an issue or trying to change a regulation or law you consider unfair. You may want to change the world, but sometimes it's best to start small, with something that people can immediately understand and relate to.

2. **Choose a type.** What kind of protest works best to achieve this goal? Maybe the most appropriate means is to start a petition or to hold a sit-in or wave a sign of support or disagreement at a town meeting. Taking time to think through your idea will help its effectiveness.

3. **Consider the time and place.** The logistics of a protest are important. Where and when is best to hold the type of demonstration you're planning? You don't want to show up for a sit-in where the business is closed or plan a march in a blizzard. Larger gatherings and marches usually require city permits, which may require several weeks to obtain. (You can find information about this on your local government website or by calling local government offices.)

4. **Find your people.** Are there others in your area or online who share your views? Social media and talking with people in your community are great tools to help build momentum for your protest. When you know how much support you may have, you can plan the right kind of protest. Just remember that any strangers on the internet are still strangers in real life. Don't agree to meet with someone you don't know without people you trust present.

5. **Plan a theme.** Get creative! Does a certain color represent your goal? What chants and hashtags can you use to spread your message? Do you want to wear matching T-shirts or hats? What unique talent can you use—playing an instrument or DJing, gymnastics or other sports, singing or theater—that can help draw attention? Look at other protests for eye-catching inspiration.

6. **List the essentials.** What will you need to make the protest work? Poster board and markers for signs, bullhorns or portable speakers for amplification, and extra T-shirts and flyers for people who join in can all be essential. If you're having a candlelight vigil, don't forget the lighters! (Or maybe use electronic candles, because of the wind.) Make a list of what you need.

How to Start a Protest of Your Own

7. **Consider your safety.** With any protest, you'll probably encounter opposing points of view. Sometimes things can get heated. Consider the possibilities of confrontation. It's OK not to engage or argue with someone. Are there people to turn to or places to go if things escalate? Plan for the safety of your fellow protesters and yourself by noting exit routes, emergency phone numbers, and other forms of support. Have a backup plan or several. If your protest is online, make sure you protect your mental health by blocking any trolls, and find a friend who can take over if things get to be too much.

8. **Know your rights.** Protesting on public property is a right, but certain regulations must be followed. Protesting on private property can be more complex and may lead to forcible removal. Civil disobedience opens you up to the possibility of arrest. Know what you may be in for by researching your rights. The ACLU has a guide to protesters' rights at ACLU.org.

9. **Promote your protest.** Use those hashtags to raise awareness on social media. Print flyers to hand out and posters to hang. Ask people with lots of followers to help spread the word. If you're looking for media coverage, how about reaching out to reporters through social media or email and inviting them to the protest?

10. **Keep the momentum going!** Don't let things die down after the protest if you don't immediately see the change you seek. Collect emails or phone numbers, and send out updates on any progress or plans for future actions. Form social media groups and encourage people to post and share related articles or news. Plan meetups to brainstorm ways to keep the issue in peoples' minds.

Above all, be brave and exercise your right to express yourself in any way you see fit. You have the power to change the world.

SOURCE NOTES

6 Louis Sahagun, "East L.A., 1968: 'Walkout!' The Day High School Students Helped Ignite the Chicano Power Movement," *Los Angeles Times*, March 1, 2018.

7 Kyle Stokes, "50 Years Ago, Thousands Walked out of East LA Schools. Now, They Say 'the Fight Isn't Over,'" *KPCC* (Pasadena, CA), March 1, 2018.

7 Stokes.

27 Eric Loomis, *A History of America in Ten Strikes* (New York: New Press, 2018), 66.

27 William J. Adelman, "The Haymarket Affair," Illinois Labor History Society, accessed August 10, 2019, http://www.illinoislaborhistory.org/the -haymarket-affair.

29 Elizabeth Cady Stanton, "Address on Woman's Rights," *Voices of Democracy* 2 (2007), https:// voicesofdemocracy.umd.edu/wp-content /uploads/2010/07/southard-stanton.pdf.

29 "Program: Woman Suffrage Procession," Washington, DC, March 3, 1913, https://www.loc .gov/item/rbpe.20801600/.

33 "Right to Peaceful Assembly: United States." Law Library of Congress, accessed August 8, 2019, https://www.loc.gov/law/help/peaceful-assembly /us.php.

34 Terance McArdle, "The Day 30,000 White Supremacists in KKK Robes Marched in the Nation's Capital," *Washington Post*, August 11, 2018.

34 McArdle.

35 Philip Bump, "The Day the Ku Klux Klan Took Over Pennsylvania Avenue," *Washington Post*, May 6, 2016, https://www.washingtonpost.com /news/the-fix/wp/2016/05/06/the-day-the-ku-klux -klan-took-over-pennsylvania-avenue/.

38 "The Bonus March (May–July, 1932)," *American Experience*, accessed August 8, 2019, http://www .pbs.org/wgbh/americanexperience/features /macarthur-bonus-march-may-july-1932/.

39 Patrick Kiger, "Eleanor Roosevelt and the Bonus Marchers," *Boundary Stones* (blog), September 8, 2014, https://blogs.weta.org/boundarystones/2014 /09/08/eleanor-roosevelt-and-bonus-marchers.

39 Paul Dickson and Thomas B. Allen, "Marching on History," *Smithsonian*, February 2003, https:// www.smithsonianmag.com/history/marching-on -history-75797769/.

42 C. Stephen Byrum, *Tennessee County History Series: McMinn County* (Memphis: Memphis State University Press, 1984).

47 Wayne Greenhaw, "Parks Felt 'Determination Cover My Body Like a Quilt,'" *CNN*, October 25, 2005, http://www.cnn.com/2005/US/10/25/parks .greenhaw/.

47 Timothy Patrick McCarthy and John McMillan, *Protest Nation: Words That Inspired a Century of American Radicalism* (New York: New Press, 2010), 71.

49 McCarthy and McMillan.

51 Fred Shuttlesworth, "Birmingham Manifesto," The Martin Luther King, Jr. Research and Education Institute, accessed August 9, 2019, https://kinginstitute.stanford.edu/encyclopedia /birmingham-campaign.

52 "Birmingham and the Children's March," *PBS*, April 26, 2013, http://www.pbs.org/black-culture /explore/civil-rights-movement-birmingham -campaign/.

55 "March on Washington for Jobs and Freedom," The Martin Luther King, Jr. Research and Education Institute, accessed August 10, 2019, https://kinginstitute.stanford.edu/encyclopedia /march-washington-jobs-and-freedom.

56 Thomas F. Jackson, *From Civil Rights to Human Rights: Martin Luther King, Jr., and the Struggle for Economic Justice* (Philadelphia: University of Pennsylvania Press, 2009), 179.

56 Richard Reeves, *President Kennedy: Profile of Power* (New York: Simon & Schuster, 1993), 583.

61 "Latino Americans: Farmworkers Strike," *PBS*, September 13, 2013, https://www.pbs.org/video /latino-americans-farmworkers-strike/.

66 Lily Rothman, "This Photo Shows the Vietnam Draft-Card Burning That Started a Movement," *Time*, October 15, 2015, https://time.com/4061835 /david-miller-draft-card/.

66 Rothman.

67 Katie Mettler, "The Day Anti-Vietnam War Protesters Tried to Levitate the Pentagon," *Washington Post*, October 19, 2017, https://www .washingtonpost.com/news/retropolis/wp/2017/10 /19/the-day-anti-vietnam-war-protesters-tried-to -levitate-the-pentagon/.

67 Mettler.

71 Danny Goldberg, "All the Human Be-In Was Saying 50 Years Ago, Was Give Peace a Chance," *Nation*, January 13, 2017, https://www.thenation .com/article/all-the-human-be-in-was-saying-50 -years-ago-was-give-peace-a-chance/.

73 Jonathan Kauffman, "Diggers Fed the Masses with 'Free' as Their Mantra," *San Francisco Chronicle*, March 10, 2017, https://www.sfchronicle .com/entertainment/article/Diggers-fed-the -masses-with-free-as-their-10987583.php.

76 "No More Miss America," press release, Redstockings, August 22, 1968, https://www .redstockings.org/index.php/no-more-miss -america.

76 "Miss America Up against the Wall," Prelinger Archives, accessed August 12, 2019, https:// archive.org/details/upagainstthewallmissamerica.

77 Robin Morgan, "I Was There: The 1968 Miss America Pageant Protest," History.com, September 7, 2018, https://www.history.com /news/miss-america-protests-1968.

81 Martha Biondi, *The Black Revolution on Campus* (Berkeley: University of California Press, 2012), 56.

88 David Carter, *Stonewall: The Riots That Sparked the Gay Revolution* (New York: St. Martin's, 2010), 137.

88 Carter, 151.

89 Carter, 176.

92 *We Hold the Rock*, YouTube video, 25:39, posted by Golden Gate National Recreation Area, October 7, 2014, https://www.youtube.com/watch?v=gEmae2PsWJI.

93 *We Hold the Rock*.

98 "Unveiling the Long-Hidden Story of the Attica Prison Takeover," *PBS News Hour*, December 21, 2016, https://www.pbs.org/newshour/show/unveiling-long-hidden-story-attica-prison-takeover.

99 "Remember Attica," *Harvard Crimson*, December 18, 1973, https://www.thecrimson.com/article/1973/12/18/remember-attica-pbwbhen-nelson-a-rockefeller/.

102 "We Shall Remain, Episode 5: Wounded Knee," *American Experience*, PBS video, aired May 11, 2009, https://www.pbs.org/wgbh/americanexperience/films/weshallremain/.

103 Emily Chertoff, "Occupy Wounded Knee: A 71-Day Siege and a Forgotten Civil Rights Movement," *Atlantic*, October 23, 2012.

106 Paul L. Montgomery, "Throngs Fill Manhattan to Protest Nuclear Weapons," *New York Times*, June 13, 1982, https://www.nytimes.com/1982/06/13/world/throngs-fill-manhattan-to-protest-nuclear-weapons.html.

106 Montgomery.

106 Ronald Reagan, "Interview with Foreign Television Journalists," Ronald Reagan Presidential Library, May 19, 1988, https://www.reaganlibrary.gov/research/speeches/051988a.

107 Mark Sinclair, "The Untold Story of the Peace Sign," *Fast Company*, October 2, 2014.

109 Lena Williams, "200,000 March in Capital to Seek Gay Rights and Money for AIDS," *New York Times*, October 12, 1987, https://www.nytimes.com/1987/10/12/us/200000-march-in-capital-to-seek-gay-rights-and-money-for-aids.html.

110 Gilbert Baker, *Rainbow Warrior: My Life in Color* (Chicago: Chicago Review Press, 2019), 33.

112 "ACT-UP Chants," ACTUPny.org, accessed October 1, 2019, https:actupny.org/documents/newmem5.html.

113 Neda Ulaby, "'Gotta Give 'Em Hope': The Legacy of Harvey Milk," *NPR*, November 11, 2008, https://www.npr.org/templates/story/story.php?storyId=96865519.

116 Zosha Millman, "19 Years Later: Looking Back at the Battle of Seattle, the WTO Riots," *Seattle Post-Intelligencer*, November 30, 2018.

116 "Lives Collide during the 1999 Seattle WTO Protests," *Leonard Lopate Show*, WNYC, February 8, 2016.

119 Phyllis Bennis, "February 15, 2003. The Day the World Said No to War," Institute for Policy Studies, February 15, 2013, https://ips-dc.org/february_15_2003_the_day_the_world_said_no_to_war/.

119 Ishaan Tharoor, "Viewpoint: Why Was the Biggest Protest in World History Ignored?," *Time*, February 15, 2013, http://world.time.com/2013/02/15/viewpoint-why-was-the-biggest-protest-in-world-history-ignored/.

119 Patrick E. Tyler, "A New Power in the Streets," *New York Times*, February 17, 2003, https://www.nytimes.com/2003/02/17/world/threats-and-responses-news-analysis-a-new-power-in-the-streets.html.

121 Patrick Barkham, "Iraq War 10 Years On: Mass Protest That Defined a Generation," *Guardian* (US edition), February 15, 2013, https://www.theguardian.com/world/2013/feb/15/iraq-war-mass-protest.

121 Tharoor, "Viewpoint."

123 "Thousands March for Immigrant Rights," *CNN*, May 1, 2006, http://www.cnn.com/2006/US/05/01/immigrant.day/.

123 Livia Gershon, "When Did May Day Turn into an Immigrants' Rights Day?," *Jstor Daily*, May 1, 2017, https://daily.jstor.org/when-did-may-day-turn-into-an-immigrants-rights-day/.

123 Dan Glaister and Ewen MacAskill, "US Counts Cost of Day without Immigrants," *Guardian* (US edition), May 1, 2006, https://www.theguardian.com/world/2006/may/02/usa.topstories3.

123 Randal C. Archibold, "Immigrants Take to U.S. Streets in Show of Strength," *New York Times*, May 2, 2006, https://www.nytimes.com/2006/05/02/us/02immig.html.

124 Glaister and MacAskill, "Day without Immigrants."

124 Sarah Aziza, "Meet the Organizers behind the Next 'Day without an Immigrant' Strike," Truthout, April 22, 2017, https://truthout.org/articles/meet-the-organizers-behind-the-next-day-without-an-immigrant-strike/.

125 Lorraine Smith Pangle, *The Political Philosophy of Benjamin Franklin* (Baltimore: Johns Hopkins University Press, 2007), 178.

127 Eric Etheridge, "Rick Santelli: Tea Party Time," *New York Times*, Opinionator, February 20, 2009, https://opinionator.blogs.nytimes.com/2009/02/20/rick-santelli-tea-party-time/.

128 "More Chicago Tea Party!!!," *Backyard Conservative* (blog), February 27, 2009, http://backyardconservative.blogspot.com/2009/02/more-chicago-tea-party.html.

131 Manuel Castells, *Networks of Outrage and Hope: Social Movements in the Internet Age* (Cambridge, UK: Polity, 2012), 163.

132 "Occupy Wall Street: A Protest Timeline," *Week*, November 21, 2011, https://theweek.com /articles/481160/occupy-wall-street-protest -timeline.

132 Inae Oh, "#OccupyWallStreet Signs and Posters," HuffPost, October 6, 2011, https://www .huffpost.com/entry/occupywallstreet -signs-an_n_998099.

133 Heather Gautney, "What Is Occupy Wall Street? The History of Leaderless Movements," *Washington Post*, October 10, 2011.

135 Barack Obama, "Remarks by the President on Trayvon Martin," Obama White House Archives, July 19, 2013, https://obamawhitehouse.archives .gov/the-press-office/2013/07/19/remarks -president-trayvon-martin.

136 "Herstory," Black Lives Matter, accessed September 27, 2019, https://blacklivesmatter.com /herstory/.

137 Charles Pulliam-Moore and Margaret Myers, "Timeline of Events in Ferguson," *PBS News Hour*, August 20, 2014, https://www.pbs.org /newshour/nation/timeline-events-ferguson.

137 Pulliam-Moore and Myers.

137 Brent McDonald, "Ferguson Shooting: A Protest Ignited," Times video, *New York Times*, August 16, 2014, https://www.nytimes.com/video/us /100000003059659/a-protest-ignited.html.

137 Shannon Luibrand, "How a Death in Ferguson Sparked a Movement in America," *CBS News*, August 7, 2015, https://cbsnews.com/news/how -the-black-lives-matter-movement-changed -america-one-year-later.

139 Bill McKibben, "A Call to Arms: An Invitation to Demand Action on Climate Change," *Rolling Stone*, May 21, 2014, https://www.rollingstone .com/politics/politics-news/a-call-to-arms-an -invitation-to-demand-action-on-climate-change -92885/.

140 Jessica Elgot, "Semi-Naked Climate Protesters Disrupt Brexit Debate," *Guardian* (US edition), April 1, 2019, https://www.theguardian.com/world /2019/apr/01/semi-naked-climate-protesters -disrupt-brexit-debate.

140 "About Us," People's Climate Movement, accessed August 19, 2019, https://peoplesclimate .org/our-movement/.

141 Amanda Holpuch, "People's Climate March: Thousands Demand Action around the World—As It Happened," *Guardian* (US edition), September 21, 2014, https://www.theguardian.com/environment /live/2014/sep/21/peoples-climate-march-live.

143 "Stop the Dakota Access Pipeline," Change.org, accessed August 19, 2019, https://www.change .org/p/jo-ellen-darcy-stop-the-dakota-access -pipeline?source_location=movement.

144 Carla Javier, "A Timeline of the Year of Resistance at Standing Rock," Splinter, December 14, 2016, https://splinternews.com/a-timeline-of-the-year -of-resistance-at-standing-rock-1794269727.

144 Javier.

147 Teresa Shook, Facebook, November 19, 2018.

148 Alanna Vagianos and Damon Dahlen, "89 Badass Feminist Signs from the Women's March on Washington," HuffPost, January 21, 2017, https://www.huffpost.com/entry/89-badass -feminist-signs-from-the-womens-march-on -washington_n_5883ea28e4b070d8cad310cd.

148 Anemona Hartocollis and Yamiche Alcindor, "Women's March Highlights as Huge Crowds Protest Trump: 'We're Not Going Away,'" *New York Times*, January 21, 2017, https://www .nytimes.com/2017/01/21/us/womens-march.html.

148 Hartocollis and Alcindor.

149 "Our Story," Pussyhat Project, accessed August 19, 2019, https://www.pussyhatproject.com/our-story.

151 Amy Spitalnick, "Charlottesville's White Supremacists Are Being Targeted by a Law That Took Down the KKK," *NBC News*, August 12, 2019, https://www.nbcnews.com/think/opinion /charlottesville-s-white-supremacists-are-being -targeted-law-took-down-ncna1041246.

151 Chris Graham, "Nazi Salutes and White Supremacism: Who Is Richard Spencer, the 'Racist Academic' behind the 'Alt Right' Movement," *Telegraph* (London), November 22, 2016, https:// www.telegraph.co.uk/news/0/richard-spencer -white-nationalist-leading-alt-right-movement/.

152 Joe Heim, "Recounting a Day of Rage, Hate, Violence and Death," *Washington Post*, August 14, 2017, https://www.washingtonpost.com /graphics/2017/local/charlottesville-timeline/.

153 Heim.

156 Kelly-Leigh Cooper, "In Florida Aftermath, US Students Say 'Never Again,'" *BBC News*, February 18, 2018, https://www.bbc.com/news /world-us-canada-43105699.

156 CNN staff, "Florida Student Emma Gonzalez to Lawmakers and Gun Advocates: 'We Call BS,'" *CNN*, February 17, 2018, https://www.cnn.com /2018/02/17/us/florida-student-emma-gonzalez -speech/index.html.

156–157 Mark Joseph Stern, "Tomorrow Is the Beginning of Democracy," Slate, March 25, 2018, https:// slate.com/news-and-politics/2018/03/the-parkland -activists-want-to-stop-gun-violence-and-they -want-to-fix-democracy.html.

157 Claudia Eller, "Emma Gonzalez Opens Up about How Her Life Has Changed since Parkland Tragedy," *Variety*, October 10, 2018, https://variety .com/2018/politics/features/emma-gonzalez -parkland-interview-1202972485/.

RECOMMENDED READING

Kauffman, L. A. *How to Read a Protest: The Art of Organizing and Resistance.* Oakland: University of California Press, 2018
Focusing on women activists and the Women's Marches, this book takes a sweeping look at the history of protest.

Loomis, Erik. *A History of America in Ten Strikes.* New York: New Press, 2018.
A clear-eyed view of the major labor struggles that helped shape the country.

Reed, T. V. *The Art of Protest: Culture and Activism from the Civil Rights Movement to the Present.* 2nd ed. Minneapolis: University of Minnesota Press, 2019.
This comprehensive guide shows how art and culture are woven into protests and demonstrations.

Siegler, Bonnie. *Signs of Resistance: A Visual History of Protest in America.* New York: Artisan, 2018.
A survey of US political art from Benjamin Franklin's cartoons through the Resistance.

Young, Ralph. *Make Art Not War: Political Protest Posters from the Twentieth Century.* New York: New York University Press, 2016.
From artistic masterpiece to handmade announcement, this collection shows the colorful breadth of resistance posters.

Zinn, Howard, and Rebecca Stefoff. *A Young People's History of the United States.* New York: Triangle Square, 2009.
A guide to US history from the point of view of immigrants, indigenous peoples, former slaves, and ethnic minorities.

INDEX

PHOTO ACKNOWLEDGMENTS

Image credits: Wikimedia Commons (Public Domain), pp. 10, 30, 38; Stock Montage/Getty Images, p. 13; Library of Congress, pp. 15, 16, 23, 27, 28, 34–35, 39 (bottom), 56, 63 (top), 64, 68; Time Inc. Picture Collection/ The LIFE Images Collection via Getty Images, p. 18 (bottom); Corbis/Getty Images, pp. 19, 54, 116; The Print Collector/Getty Images, p. 20; The Oakland History Room, Oakland Public Library, p. 24; Bettmann Archive/ Getty Images, pp. 26, 27, 48, 60, 76, 80, 83, 92, 94, 96, 100, 102, 112, 113; Jack Benton/Getty Images, p. 32; National Archives (593253), p. 36; Courtesy of University of Pittsburgh (public domain), p. 39 (top); Courtesy of Tennessee State Library and Archives, pp. 40, 42; Grey Villet/The LIFE Picture Collection/Getty Images, p. 44; Underwood Archives/Getty Images, p. 47; Frank Rockstroh/Michael Ochs Archives/Getty Images, pp. 50, 53; Paul Slade/Paris Match/Getty Images, p. 57; Francis Miller/The LIFE Picture Collection/Getty Images, pp. 58–59; Frank Lennon/Toronto Star/Getty Images, p. 62; Arthur Schatz/The LIFE Picture/Getty Images, p. 63 (bottom); Fairfax Media/Getty Images, p. 66; Bernie Boston/The Washington Post/Getty Images, p. 67; The Frent Collection/Getty Images, p. 69 (all); Ralph Crane/The LIFE Picture Collection/Getty Images, p. 70; Blank Archives/Archive Photos/ Getty Images, p. 73; Bev Grant/Getty Images, pp. 74, 75; David Fenton/Getty Images, p. 78; Paul Connell/The Boston Globe/Getty Images, p. 85; Ben Hider/Getty Images, p. 86; NY Daily News Archive/Getty Images, p. 87; Charles Ruppmann/NY Daily News/Getty Images, pp. 90–91; Dan Farrell/NY Daily News Archive/Getty Images, p. 98; Lee Frey/Authenticated News International/Getty Images, p. 104; JARNOUX Patrick/Paris Match/Getty Images, p. 107; jean-Louis Atlan/Sygma/Getty Images, p. 108; werk4peace/flickr, p. 110; Andrew Lichtenstein/Corbis/Getty Images, p. 114; Marco Di Lauro/Getty Images, p. 118; Steve Russell/Toronto Star/Getty Images, p. 120; David S. Holloway/ Getty Images, p. 122; Aydin Palabiyikoglu/Anadolu Agency/Getty Images, p. 124; Manny Crisostomo/Sacramento Bee/MCT/Getty Images, p. 126; Bill Clark/Roll Call/Getty Images, p. 128; Gage Skidmore/Wikimedia Commons (CC by 2.0), p. 129; STAN HONDA/AFP/Getty Images, p. 130; Monika Graff/Getty Images, p. 133; Scott Olson/Getty Images, pp. 134, 138, 143; EITAN ABRAMOVICH/AFP/Getty Images, p. 138; Keith Getter/Moment Mobile/Getty Images, p. 139; NICHOLAS KAMM/AFP/Getty Images, p. 142; MARK RALSTON/AFP/Getty Images, p. 144; flickr, p. 146; Molly Adams/ flickr (CC BY 2.0), p. 148; Daniel Oberhaus (2017)/flickr (CC BY 2.0), p. 149; Zach D Roberts/NurPhoto/Getty Images, p. 150; GrammarGirl/flickr (CC BY 2.0), p. 154; Dimitrios Kambouris/Getty Images, p. 155; Fibonacci Blue/flickr (CC by 2.0), p. 157. Design elements: Cafe Racer/Shutterstock.com; Eugene Ivanov/Shutterstock.com; Milan M/Shutterstock. com; Doctor Letters/Shutterstock.com.

Cover: Cafe Racer/Shutterstock.com; Eugene Ivanov/Shutterstock.com; Milan M/Shutterstock.com; Doctor Letters/ Shutterstock.com.

ABOUT THE AUTHOR

Marke Bieschke is the publisher of the *San Francisco Bay Guardian* and 48 Hills. He serves on the board of the GLBT Historical Society and writes about gay issues for several international publications. Formerly, he edited Gay.com and PlanetOut.com. Marke lives in San Francisco with his husband, David.

Photo credit: Mona Caron